SMP 11-16

Book Y5

D0431365

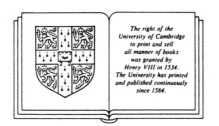

The right of the
University of Cambridge
to print and sell
all manner of books
was granted by
Henry VIII in 1534.
The University has printed
and published continuously
since 1584.

Cambridge University Press

Cambridge
New York   Port Chester
Melbourne   Sydney

Published by the Press Syndicate of the University of Cambridge
The Pitt Building, Trumpington Street, Cambridge CB2 1RP
40 West 20th Street, New York, NY 10011, USA
10 Stamford Road, Oakleigh, Melbourne 3166, Australia

First published 1987
Third printing 1990

Illustrations by Dick Bonson, Chris Evans and David Parkins
Photographs by John Ling and Paul Scruton
Cover photograph by Nigel Luckhurst of a globe showing the Fuller
Projection which was designed by Buckminster Fuller and Shoji
Sadao Cartographers
Diagrams and phototypesetting by Parkway Group, London
and Abingdon, and Gecko Limited, Bicester

Printed in Great Britain at the University Press, Cambridge

British Library cataloguing in publication data
SMP 11–16 yellow series.
  Bk Y5
    1. Mathematics – 1961–
    I. School Mathematics Project
    510   QA39.2
    ISBN 0 521 31477 1

Contents

1 Surfaces

A Developable surfaces: the cylinder

Roughly speaking, a **developable** surface is one we can make out of a piece of paper, without stretching the paper at all.

For example, the label on a soup tin starts as a rectangle. It is printed while it is still flat. Then it is wrapped round the tin and becomes a cylinder. So the curved surface of a cylinder is a developable surface.

In the process the paper is curved but the design and the letters are not distorted. Three things stay the same or, as we say, are **preserved**.

1 **Distances** in any direction are preserved.

In fact, the circumference of the cylinder is just the length of the rectangle (assuming no overlap), and the height of the cylinder is the height of the rectangle.

2 **Angles** are preserved.

For example, the two angles shown here are right-angles on the flat rectangle, and they still remain right-angles on the cylinder.

3 **Areas** are preserved.

The coloured area is exactly the same on the cylinder as it is on the flat rectangle.

In fact, the curved surface of the whole cylinder is the same area as the rectangle, again assuming no overlap.

Suppose a tin can has a diameter of 72 mm.
A rectangle which just wraps round it with no overlap must have a length equal to the circumference of the tin, that is $\pi \times 72\,\text{mm} = 226\,\text{mm}$ (to the nearest mm).

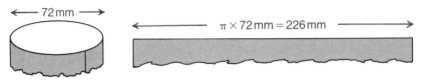

72 mm

$\pi \times 72\,\text{mm} = 226\,\text{mm}$

A1 Calculate the length of a rectangle which will just wrap round a cylindrical tin of diameter 80 mm.

A2 A rectangle of length 60 mm is rolled into a cylinder. Calculate the diameter of the cylinder.

The helix

Draw a straight line on a rectangular piece of paper. Roll the rectangle into a cylinder.

The line becomes part of a curve called a **helix**.

The helix can be seen in many places, for example

a bolt, 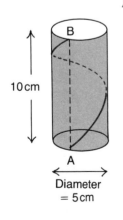 a twisted strip of paper.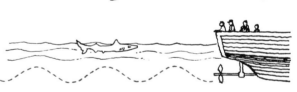

It is also the path of a tip of a ship's propeller as the ship moves along at a steady speed.

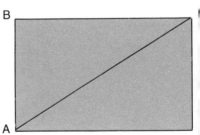

A3 The diagram on the left shows a helix which goes exactly once round a cylinder. The point B is directly above A.

10 cm

B

A

Diameter = 5 cm

If the cylinder is cut along AB and flattened into a rectangle, the helix becomes a diagonal of the rectangle.

B

A

(a) Calculate the length of the rectangle.

(b) Draw the rectangle with its diagonal full size. Cut it out. Make it into a cylinder.

(c) Use Pythagoras' rule to calculate the length of the helix. Check by measuring.

A4 Calculate the length of a helix which goes once round a cylinder of height 20 cm and diameter 9 cm.

A helix crosses every circle parallel to the base of the cylinder at the same angle.

We can find this angle by trigonometry. The next question shows how.

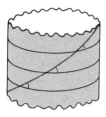

A5 A helix goes once round a cylinder of height 4 cm and diameter 3 cm.

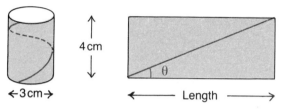

(a) The cylinder is unrolled into a rectangle. Calculate the length of the rectangle.

(b) Use trigonometry to calculate the angle marked θ.

A6 A helix goes once round a cylinder of diameter 8·5 cm and height 10·2 cm. Calculate the angle that the helix makes with the base.

A7 A helix goes once round a cylinder of **radius** 10 cm. If the helix makes an angle of 30° with the base, how high is the cylinder?

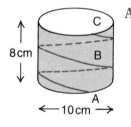

A8 Suppose a helix goes twice round a cylinder of diameter 10 cm and height 8 cm, as shown on the left.
If the cylinder is cut along ABC and flattened, we get a rectangle which looks like this.

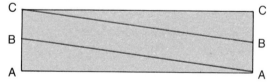

(a) Calculate the length of the helix.

(b) Calculate the angle it makes with the base.

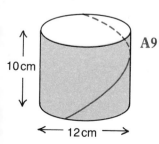

A9 The diagram on the left shows a helix which goes only halfway round a cylinder of diameter 12 cm and height 10 cm.

Draw the flattened-out cylinder and calculate the length of the helix and the angle it makes with the base.

3

A10   If this rectangle is rolled into a cylinder,

(a) how many helices will there be?

(b) how many times will each helix go round the cylinder?

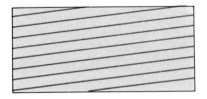

*A11   If this helical spring is straightened out, how long will the wire be?

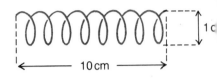

B   Shortest paths

A spider and a fly are crawling about on a gutter. The gutter is half of a cylinder, of diameter 12 cm and length 100 cm.

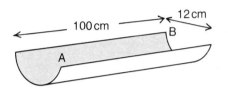

The spider is at A and the fly at B. What is the shortest path on the gutter from A to B?

To find out, we imagine the gutter unrolled into a rectangle.
The shortest path must be along the diagonal AB.

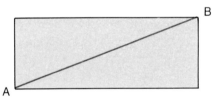

On the actual gutter the diagonal becomes a helix, but it must still be the shortest path.
If there were an even shorter path on the gutter this would correspond to a path on the rectangle shorter than the diagonal, because all distances are preserved when the gutter is unrolled. But there can be no shorter path than the diagonal.

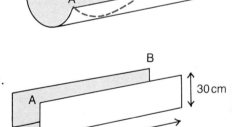

B1   This time the spider and fly are on the square-section gutter shown here.

Find the length of the shortest path on the gutter from A to B.

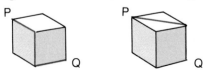

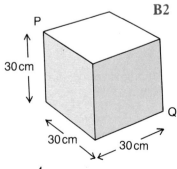

B2   Now they are at opposite corners P, Q of a cube of side 30 cm. Two possible paths on the cube from P to Q are shown below.

The second is shorter than the first, but can still be improved on. Find the length of the shortest path. How many shortest paths are there?

B3 The diagrams below show a cuboid 5 cm by 6 cm by 3 cm, and a net for it.

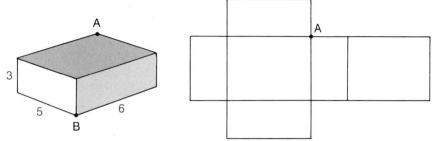

(a) Draw the net (a sketch will do) and mark the point A as shown. There are **three** points on the net corresponding to B on the cuboid. Mark each of them with a B.

(b) On your diagram show a straight path from B to A which crosses over a 6 cm edge. Calculate the length of this path.

(c) There are two straight paths from B to A which cross over a 5 cm edge. Draw them both and calculate their lengths.

(d) What is the shortest distance from B to A on the surface of the cuboid?

B4 A and B are on opposite sides of a long cylinder of diameter 30 cm.

A is 10 cm from one end of the cylinder and B is 20 cm from the end.

Calculate the length of the shortest path on the cylinder from A to B.

(Imagine the cylinder is cut and flattened out.)

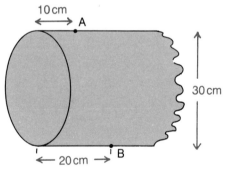

B5 Find the length of the shortest path from P to Q on this cylinder.

(Calculate the distance from R to S first. What fraction of the circumference is it?)

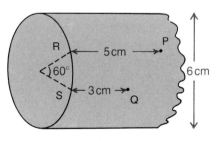

*B6 Repeat question B4, but this time the cylinder is an open-ended cardboard tube with A on the outside but B on the **inside**.

C Developable surfaces: the cone

Draw a circle of radius 4 cm.

Draw two lines from the centre, at right-angles to each other.

Cut out the shape shown here.
It is a **sector** of the circle. The angle of the sector is 270°.

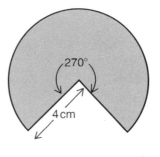

By placing the two straight edges together, make the sector into a **cone**.

The radius of the sector, 4 cm, becomes the **slant height** of the cone.

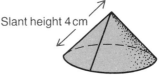

The base of the cone is a circle.

The circumference of the base . . . . . . is equal to the length of the **arc** of the sector . . . . . . which is ¾ of the circumference of the circle with radius 4 cm.

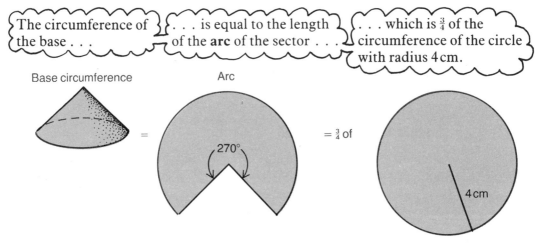

Base circumference

Arc

C1 (a) Calculate the circumference of the circle with radius 4 cm.

(b) Calculate the length of the arc of the 270° sector of this circle.

(c) The answer to (b) is the base circumference of the cone.
Divide it by 2π to find the base radius of the cone.

You should find that the base radius of the cone is ¾ of the radius of the sector (¾ of 4 cm).

If you think about it, this is the result you would expect. The base circumference is ¾ of the larger circle's circumference, so the base radius will be ¾ of the larger circle's radius.

(The circumference of a circle is directly proportional to its radius.)

We get a similar result when the sector has a different angle.

This sector is ⅓ of a circle of radius 6 cm.

When the sector is made into a cone the base radius will be ⅓ of 6 cm, or 2 cm.

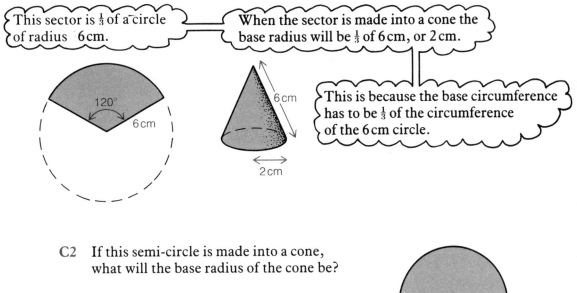

This is because the base circumference has to be ⅓ of the circumference of the 6 cm circle.

C2 If this semi-circle is made into a cone, what will the base radius of the cone be?

C3 (a) What fraction of a complete circle is this sector?

(b) If the sector is made into a cone, what will the base radius of the cone be?

We can use the same idea 'in reverse' to calculate the angle of the sector given the slant height and base radius of the cone.

In this cone the base radius is $\frac{6}{10}$ of the slant height.

So the cone is made from $\frac{6}{10}$ of a circle of radius 10 cm.

The angle of the sector is $\frac{6}{10}$ of 360° = **216°**.

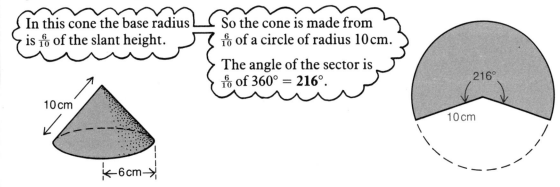

C4 Calculate the angle of the sector needed to make a cone with

(a) base radius 4 cm and slant height 5 cm

(b) base radius 10 cm and slant height 18 cm

(c) base radius 0·4 cm and slant height 2 cm

Shortest paths on a cone

A termite has found its way blocked by a conical ant-hill. The termite is at A and needs to crawl to the diametrically opposite point B. What is the shortest possible path?

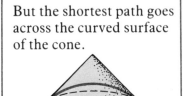

1 m

A   B

← 0·7 m →

| A path round the base has length $\frac{1}{2} \times 2\pi \times 0.7$ m, or about 2·2 m.
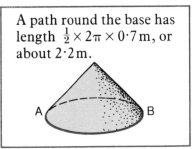
A   B | A path over the top has a length of 2 m.
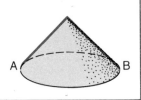
A   B | But the shortest path goes across the curved surface of the cone.
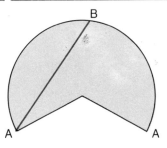
A   B |

Imagine the cone is made of paper. If it is cut through A and flattened out, we get a sector.

The shortest path from A to B on the sector is also the shortest path on the cone, because distances are preserved when the cone is flattened out. On the cone itself, this path is a curve.

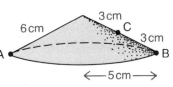

B

A   A

C5 (a) Calculate the angle of the sector above.

     (b) Using a scale of 5 cm to 1 m, make a scale drawing of the sector. Find the length of AB to the nearest 0·1 m.

C6 By making a drawing, find the shortest distance on this cone

     (a) from A to B   (b) from A to C

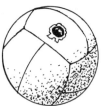

3 cm
6 cm   C
         3 cm
A   B
← 5 cm →

D   Non-developable surfaces: the sphere

The sphere is not a developable surface. A sphere cannot be made by cutting and bending paper.

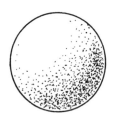

The spherical balls shown below can be made out of rubber, leather or plastic pieces. But even if the pieces are flat to start with, when the ball is inflated they will be **stretched** and distorted. A sphere cannot be made from paper which will not stretch.

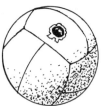

Shortest paths on a sphere

It is useful to have a ball or globe to help you in what follows.

1 Imagine a hill in the shape of a hemisphere (half-sphere). You are at a point A at the base, and you want to get to the top, B.

The shortest path from A to B will be the path which goes 'straight up' the hill, as shown in the diagram.

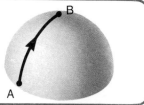

2 Now suppose you start from a point C which is some way up the hill from the base. As before you want to get to the top, B.

Once again, the shortest path from C to B will go 'straight up' the hill, as shown in this diagram.

3 Now imagine that you go along the shortest path from C to B and then continue over the top, without turning to the left or the right.

You will arrive at the point diametrically opposite A on the base.

4 If the hemisphere is part of a whole sphere, and you continue along the path, you will make a complete circle and arrive back at C.

The shortest path from C to B is part of the complete circle.

The circle in the last diagram is an example of a **great circle**.

A great circle is **any** circle on a sphere which divides the sphere into two hemispheres.

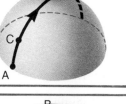

The shortest path between any two points P and Q on a sphere is part of a great circle.

If you imagine turning the sphere until Q is at the top, this fact becomes obvious.

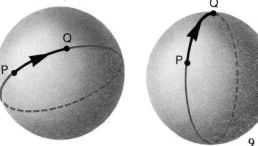

The centre of a great circle is at the centre of the sphere itself.
The radius of a great circle is the radius of the sphere.

The shortest path between two points A and B is part of
a great circle. To calculate the length of the path, we
need to know the radius of the sphere and what fraction
of a great circle the path is.

To find the fraction we need to know the size of the
angle AOB, where O is the centre of the sphere.

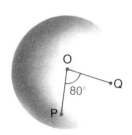

Worked example

Calculate the length of the shortest path from A to B in the diagram
above, if the radius of the sphere is 50 cm and the angle AOB is 110°.

The total length of the great circle is $2\pi \times 50$ cm.

The total circumference
gives an angle of 360°
at the centre.

The arc AB is $\frac{110}{360}$ of
the total circumference.

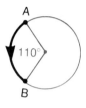

So the length of the arc AB is $\frac{110}{360} \times 2\pi \times 50$ cm = **96 cm** (to the nearest cm).

The distance by the shortest path is called the **great circle distance**.

D1 P and Q are two points on the surface
of a sphere of radius 1 m.
O is the centre of the sphere, and the
angle POQ is 80°.

Calculate the great circle distance from
P to Q.

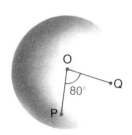

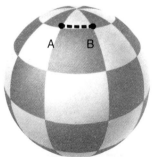

D2 An ant crawls from A to B on the surface
of this spherical ball. Did it go by the
shortest path from A to B? Explain the
reason for your answer.

D3 The great circle distance from London to New York is 3460 miles.
The radius of the Earth is 3960 miles.
If lines are drawn from London to the Earth's centre and from New York
to the Earth's centre, calculate the angle between them.

2 Optimisation

A 'Bin-packing' problems

A1 There are 200 people at a conference who are to go on a coach trip.
Each coach has 50 passenger seats.
It is a very simple matter to work out that 4 coaches are needed.

Now suppose we change the problem by adding some restrictions.
The 200 people come from the following countries:

29 French	26 German	31 American	27 Canadian
20 Italian	18 Japanese	24 British	25 Dutch

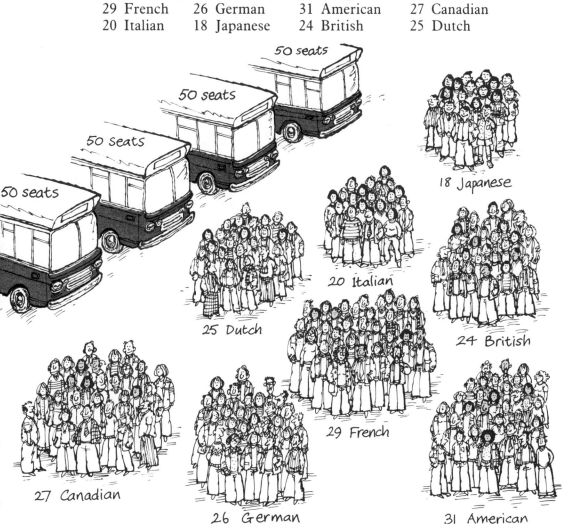

People of the same nationality must all sit together.
More than one nationality may share a coach.

Work out how many coaches are needed now.

The coach problem is an optimisation problem. ('Optimisation' means finding the best possible way of doing something.)

Coaches are expensive to hire, so the 'best' solution to the problem is one which uses the smallest number of coaches.

You may have found the problem very easy to solve, but similar problems can be much more difficult.
Here is a way to think of the problem, and other problems like it.

Think of the coaches as 'bins', each 50 units high.

Start by putting the largest amount in first, the 31 Americans.

The largest amount is more than half the capacity of the bin.
Any other amount which is more than half the capacity of a bin will need a new bin. So we need a new bin for the 29 French, for the 27 Canadians and for the 26 Germans.

Now we have some choice as to what to do next. But we cannot get all the other four amounts into the four bins we have used so far. We must use a fifth bin.

Here is one possible solution.

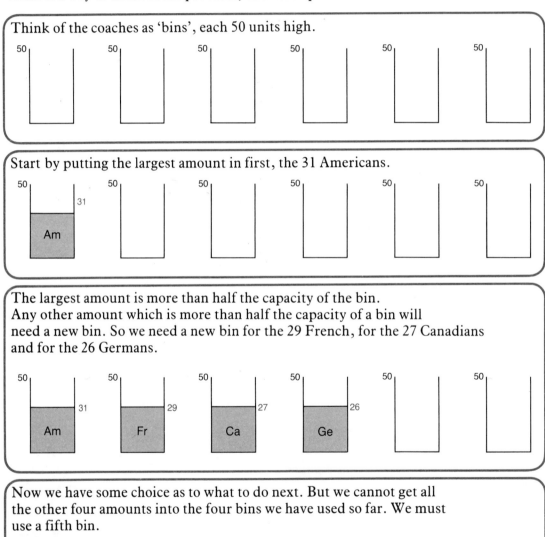

There are many other problems which can be thought of as 'bin-packing' problems.

In a 'bin-packing' problem there is often a huge number of ways of packing the items into the 'bins'. But it is not always obvious, when you have an answer, whether it is the best possible packing, that is, the one which uses the smallest number of bins.

Bin-packing problems occur in industry and commerce, where people are always looking for ways to minimise costs. Real-life packing problems often have so many items to be packed that the only way to solve the problem is to use a computer. The questions in this section involve small numbers of items. They are designed to give you a flavour of this type of problem.

The first step is to decide what the 'bins' are – it is not always clear. For example, think about this problem:

> A carpenter has a supply of planks, each 200 cm long.
> He needs to cut out pieces of the following lengths:
>
> | 145 cm | 95 cm | 92 cm | 89 cm | 71 cm |
> |--------|-------|-------|-------|-------|
> | 109 cm | 73 cm | 132 cm | 58 cm | 56 cm |
>
> What is the minimum number of planks he can use?

We can think of each plank as a 'bin' 200 units high.
The ten given lengths are the items which have to be 'packed' into the bins.

A2 (a) Solve the problem to find the minimum number of planks.

   (b) How much wood is wasted?

A3 A firm's delivery van can carry up to 2 tonnes.
   The following loads have to be carried to a customer:

Load	A	B	C	D	E	F	G	H	I	J
Weight in tonnes	1·7	1·2	0·8	1·5	0·4	0·7	0·1	1·8	0·3	1·5

   (a) What is the smallest number of journeys which will be needed to deliver all the loads?

   (b) The firm would like the last journey to be as lightly loaded as possible, to leave room for some other items. Show how this can be done.

A4 A plumber wishes to cut twelve pieces of copper pipe. They are to be cut from standard 3-metre lengths.

Piece	A	B	C	D	E	F	G	H	I	J	K	L
Length in metres	$\frac{1}{2}$	$\frac{1}{2}$	$\frac{3}{4}$	$\frac{3}{4}$	$\frac{3}{4}$	$\frac{3}{4}$	1	1	1	$1\frac{1}{2}$	$1\frac{3}{4}$	$1\frac{3}{4}$

   (a) What can you think of as the 'bins' in this problem?

   (b) What is the smallest number of 3-metre lengths the plumber can use? Show how the pieces would be cut.

A5 A TV company plans its programmes so that breaks for adverts are no longer than **2 minutes**. They have to fit in the following adverts, whose lengths are given in seconds.

Cereal	50	Cars	36	Margarine	35	Chocolate	25
Cream	50	Bread	36	Detergent	35	Newspaper	24
Sausages	50	Holidays	36	Hair spray	35	Bacon	24
Paint	50	Crisps	36	New film	32		
Tyres	36	Video	36	Tissues	32		

(a) What is the minimum number of advertising breaks needed? Show how you would make up each break (e.g. 50, 25, 24).

(b) How long is the longest advert which could be added to the list without increasing the number of breaks?

Bin-packing problems can be solved using a computer to go through all the possible ways of packing the items and to find the best way. But when the number of items is very large, the process can take a lot of computer time and be very expensive.

In practice it may not be worth trying to find the **best** solution to a problem: a good solution may be enough, if it saves computer time. The method usually used for bin-packing problems is called the 'decreasing first fit' method. It does not necessarily yield the best possible solution (the one which uses fewest bins), but it does lead to a solution which uses only up to 20% more bins than the minimum.

The basis of the method can be set out as a flowchart loop:

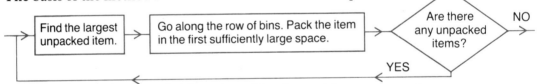

The questions below may (with patience) be done without a computer. But if you have access to a computer and are able to program it, then use it.

A6 Items of information are to be 'packed' in computer storage units. Each item of information consists of a number of characters. Each storage unit can hold up to 300 characters.

The numbers of characters in each item of information are as follows:

175	205	24	138	45.	62	18	241	215	111	106
51	24	62	189	105	77	29	43	99	162	205
9	125	176	49	58	33	149	153	122	56	92

Ideally, the number of storage units used should be as small as possible. Use the 'decreasing first fit' method to pack the items into units.

A7 Another bin-packing method is called the 'decreasing best fit' method. Instead of packing the largest unpacked item into the first large enough space, we pack it into the fullest bin it will fit into. Use this method to do question A6.

B Maximisation subject to a constraint

B1 A woman is escaping from a foreign country. She has a knapsack and can carry only a limited weight (4·0 kg).

She has a number of items which she would like to carry away with her. They have different weights and different values.

Knapsack can carry up to 4·0 kg.

Camera
weighs 2·0 kg
worth £85

Book
weighs 0·3 kg
worth £7

Alarm clock
weighs 0·8 kg
worth £25

Telescope
weighs 2·5 kg
worth £105

Radio
weighs 1·6 kg
worth £47

(a) What items should she pack to make the load as valuable as possible?

(b) What will her load be worth?

B2 Suppose the woman has several of each item instead of just one of each. The items have the same weights and values as before.

Now she has to decide, for example, **how many** telescopes to take, not whether to take a single telescope or not. And so for the other items.

(a) What should she now pack to make the load in the knapsack as valuable as possible?

(b) What will the load be worth?

In questions B1 and B2 you were asked to maximise the value of the load while at the same time making sure that the weight did not exceed 4 kg.

We say that you were trying to maximise the value, subject to the **constraint** that the weight should not exceed 4 kg. ('Constraint' is another word for 'restriction'.)

Problems of the type given in question B2 are often difficult, because you may not be sure that you have found the best possible combination of items. Perhaps there is a combination which you haven't thought of which is even better.

The only way to be sure is to have a method of going through all the possibilities. A method like this is called a **systematic** method.

We shall first describe a systematic method for solving a simpler problem, in which there are only two kinds of item.

Jim has £3 to spend on chocolate.

He has a choice of two types: Radbury's 70 g bars, costing 45p each,
Cowntree's 130 g bars, costing 80p each.

He wants to get as much chocolate as possible.

The constraint here is that the total cost must not exceed £3.

1 Start with the maximum possible number of one of the bars.
(The working is shorter if you start with the more expensive bar.)

The maximum number of Cowntree bars is **3**, because 4 would cost £3·20.

3 Cowntree bars cost £2·40, leaving enough money for **1** Radbury bar.

The weight of this combination (3 Cowntree, 1 Radbury) is **460 g**.

2 Now reduce the number of Cowntree bars by one, and find the maximum number of Radbury bars which can be bought as well.

2 Cowntree bars cost £1·60, leaving enough money for **3** Radbury bars.

The weight of this combination (2 Cowntree, 3 Radbury) is **470 g**.

3 Now reduce the number of Cowntree bars by one again. As before, find the maximum number of Radbury bars which can be bought as well. Continue until the number of Cowntree bars is 0, and the maximum possible number of Radbury bars is bought.
The results can be set out in a table.

Number of Cowntrees	Number of Radburys	Weight
3	1	460 g
2	3	470 g

{ and so on }

B3 (a) Copy this table and complete it.
(b) What is the greatest weight, and which combination gives it?

B4 A van costs £55 to hire and will carry up to 1·5 tonnes.
A lorry costs £90 to hire and will carry up to 2·5 tonnes.

Find the maximum weight which can be carried if the total hire cost must not exceed £400.

The method used so far can be extended to problems where there are three kinds of item to choose from. Here is an example.

A carpenter can make three kinds of item. This table shows the time it takes to make each one, and the amount of profit he makes.

Item	Time taken	Profit
Garden seat	$1\frac{1}{2}$ days	£15
Dining table	3 days	£60
Stool	2 days	£35

If he has a maximum of 10 days in which to work, what should he make to maximise his profit?

The constraint here is a time constraint: he has a maximum of 10 days. The most time-consuming item is the dining table. So start with the maximum possible number of those. (This shortens the working.)

	Dining tables	Stools	Garden seats	Profit
The maximum number of tables is 3, leaving no time for anything else.	3	0	0	£180
Reduce the number of tables by one. Maximise the number of stools.	2	2	0	£190
Then reduce the number of stools by one.		1	1	£170
And then by one again.		0	2	£150
Now reduce the number of tables by one again, and continue as before.	1			

B5 Complete the solution of the problem.

B6 A firm exports three kinds of machine.
Their weights and the costs of exporting them are shown in this table.

	Pneumatic drill	Grinder	Chainsaw
Weight	26 kg	12 kg	8 kg
Export cost	£72	£30	£10

A second firm is exporting an empty boiler. They offer to pack it with machines up to a weight limit of 100 kg, and carry them free. What should be packed, to save as much as possible in export costs?

The government spends a lot of money each year, on such things as education, health, defence, and so on. Much of this money comes from **income tax**. The amount which anyone has to pay depends on their income – the amount of money they have coming in.

People do not pay tax on the whole of their income. There is part of their income which they are allowed to keep without any tax being deducted from it. This part is called their **allowances**. The size of the allowances depends on a whole variety of things.

Find out

It is possible for someone to have an income and not pay any income tax.

Find out what is the most you can earn without having to pay tax.

The **rate** at which you pay tax depends on how much you earn.
Your taxable income (your income minus allowances) is 'sliced' into **tax bands**. Each band is taxed at a different rate.

This diagram shows the tax bands and tax rates in 1986–87.

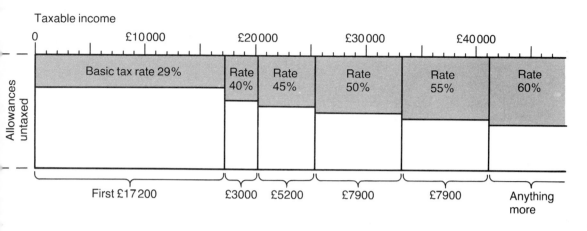

Taxable income

Find out

Find out what the tax bands are at the moment.

Work out how much tax is paid altogether by someone with a taxable income of £50000.

Tax facts

- The 'tax year' (the year for which your income is calculated for tax purposes) runs from 6th April in one year to 5th April in the next year.

  Before 1752, rents and taxes of all kinds were calculated up to the end of the first quarter of the year – 25th March, called 'Lady Day'.

  In 1752 an adjustment was made to the calendar, so that 2nd September was followed by 14th September. So from Lady Day 1752 to Lady Day 1753 there were only 354 days.
  The Treasury accounting system could not cope with that, so from 1753 taxes were collected 11 days later, on 5th April!

  When income tax was first introduced in 1799, 5th April was the date on which it was collected.

- For nearly 30 years in the 19th century there was no income tax. It started again in 1842. The rate was 3%!

- In 1875 the rate of income tax was down to 0·83%.

- The highest the (basic) rate has ever been was during the Second World War, when it was 50%.

- There are two small islands around the British Isles where no income tax is paid by the inhabitants – Lundy Island and Sark.

3 Algebraic fractions

A Sums and differences of fractions

You will be familiar with the process of 'multiplying out' an expression such as $3(a + b)$.

$$3(a + b) = 3a + 3b$$

The same kind of process can also be applied to expressions such as $\dfrac{a + b}{4}$,

because $\dfrac{a + b}{4}$ can be thought of as $\frac{1}{4}(a + b)$.

$$\frac{a + b}{4} = \tfrac{1}{4}(a + b) = \tfrac{1}{4}a + \tfrac{1}{4}b$$

But $\frac{1}{4}a + \frac{1}{4}b$ can also be written as $\dfrac{a}{4} + \dfrac{b}{4}$, so we get

$$\frac{a + b}{4} = \frac{a}{4} + \frac{b}{4}$$

This is just common sense really, as you can see if you replace a and b by numbers. For example, if you divide $40 + 8$ by 4, the result is the same as if you divide 40 by 4 and 8 by 4 and add the two answers.

There is nothing special about 4. The denominator can be any number.

$$\frac{a + b}{c} = \frac{a}{c} + \frac{b}{c}$$

Sometimes we can do some simplifying after we have 'split' a fraction in this way. For example

$$\frac{2a + 3b}{ab} = \frac{2a}{ab} + \frac{3b}{ab} \left\{ = \frac{2a}{ab} + \frac{3b}{ab} \right\} = \frac{2}{b} + \frac{3}{a}$$

What we have done here is to re-write, or **express**, the single algebraic fraction $\dfrac{2a + 3b}{ab}$ as the sum of two simpler fractions.

> **A1** Express $\dfrac{3x + 6y}{xy}$ as the sum of two fractions and simplify each of the two fractions.

> **A2** Express each of these as the sum or difference of two fractions, and simplify where possible.
>
> (a) $\dfrac{ab + ac}{bc}$ (b) $\dfrac{3p - 6q}{3pq}$ (c) $\dfrac{p^2 + q^2}{pq}$ (d) $\dfrac{3x + 1}{x}$ (e) $\dfrac{6a - 4}{2a}$

It is sometimes useful to be able to reverse this process, and replace the sum of two algebraic fractions by a single fraction.

If the denominators of the two fractions are equal, there is no difficulty.

For example, $\dfrac{a}{p} + \dfrac{2b}{p} = \dfrac{a+2b}{p}$.

But if the denominators are different, as for example in $\dfrac{2}{b} + \dfrac{3}{a}$, things are not quite so simple.

Look back at the worked example on the opposite page (above question A1).

In that example, we started with $\dfrac{2a+3b}{ab}$ and expressed it as $\dfrac{2}{b} + \dfrac{3}{a}$.

If we want to go backwards, we have to put in a step which makes the two denominators equal, like this:

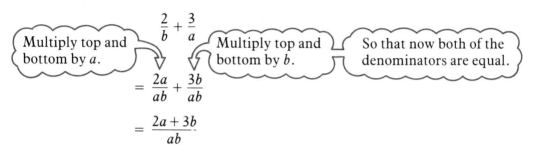

Compare this with adding two 'arithmetical' fractions, such as $\frac{2}{5} + \frac{1}{3}$.

$$\frac{2}{5} + \frac{1}{3}$$

Multiply top and bottom by 3.   Multiply top and bottom by 5.

$$= \frac{6}{15} + \frac{5}{15}$$

$$= \frac{6+5}{15} = \frac{11}{15}$$

A3   Write each of these expressions as a single algebraic fraction.

(a) $\dfrac{1}{x} + \dfrac{1}{y}$ (b) $\dfrac{1}{2} + \dfrac{1}{a}$ (c) $\dfrac{a}{b} - \dfrac{1}{c}$ (d) $\dfrac{x}{y} + \dfrac{u}{v}$ (e) $\dfrac{1}{3} - \dfrac{s}{t}$

(f) $2 + \dfrac{1}{x}$ (g) $\dfrac{1}{2a} + \dfrac{3}{b}$ (h) $\dfrac{3}{x} - 1$ (i) $\dfrac{x}{2} + \dfrac{2}{x}$ (j) $\dfrac{u}{v} - \dfrac{v}{u}$

A4   The formula $\dfrac{1}{f} = \dfrac{1}{u} + \dfrac{1}{v}$ is used in physics.

(a) Express $\dfrac{1}{u} + \dfrac{1}{v}$ as a single fraction.

(b) Re-write the formula in the form $f = \ldots$

Worked example

Express $\dfrac{x}{6} + \dfrac{4}{3y}$ as a single fraction.

We will make both denominators $6y$, because both 6 and $3y$ divide exactly into $6y$.

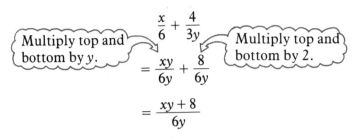

Multiply top and bottom by y.

Multiply top and bottom by 2.

$$\dfrac{x}{6} + \dfrac{4}{3y}$$

$$= \dfrac{xy}{6y} + \dfrac{8}{6y}$$

$$= \dfrac{xy + 8}{6y}$$

A5 Express $\dfrac{a}{2b} + \dfrac{c}{8}$ as a single fraction.

A6 Express each of these as a single fraction.

(a) $\dfrac{x}{3} - \dfrac{y}{12}$ (b) $\dfrac{a}{3x} + \dfrac{b}{xy}$ (c) $\dfrac{5}{a} + \dfrac{2}{ab}$ (d) $\dfrac{1}{p} - \dfrac{3}{p^2}$

A7 Express each of these as a single fraction.

(a) $\dfrac{3}{2a} + \dfrac{5}{a^2}$ (b) $\dfrac{x}{3a} + \dfrac{y}{2ab}$ (c) $\dfrac{y}{4x} - \dfrac{1}{2xy}$ (d) $\dfrac{a}{3x^2} - \dfrac{1}{xy}$

A8 The formula $\dfrac{1}{R} = \dfrac{1}{R_1} + \dfrac{1}{R_2}$ is used in electricity calculations.

(a) If R_1 is $0\cdot2$ and R_2 is $0\cdot4$, calculate the value of $\dfrac{1}{R}$, and from this the value of R.

(b) Express $\dfrac{1}{R_1} + \dfrac{1}{R_2}$ as a single fraction involving R_1 and R_2.

(c) Re-write the formula in the form $R = \ldots$

(d) Use your re-written formula to calculate R when R_1 is $0\cdot2$ and R_2 is $0\cdot4$, and check that the answer agrees with your answer to part (a).

A9 u, v and f are connected by the formula $\dfrac{1}{u} + \dfrac{1}{v} = \dfrac{1}{f}$.

u, v and m are connected by the formula $v = mu$.

Show that $\dfrac{1}{f} = \dfrac{m+1}{mu}$, and write a formula for u in terms of f and m.

Worked example

Express $\dfrac{3}{x+1} + \dfrac{4}{x+2}$ as a single fraction.

We make both denominators $(x+1)(x+2)$.

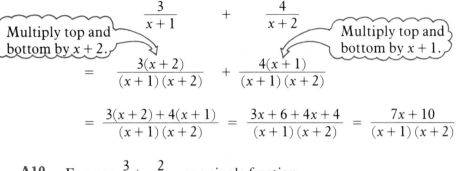

$$= \frac{3(x+2)}{(x+1)(x+2)} + \frac{4(x+1)}{(x+1)(x+2)}$$

$$= \frac{3(x+2)+4(x+1)}{(x+1)(x+2)} = \frac{3x+6+4x+4}{(x+1)(x+2)} = \frac{7x+10}{(x+1)(x+2)}$$

A10   Express $\dfrac{3}{x} + \dfrac{2}{x+1}$ as a single fraction.

A11   Express each of these as a single fraction.

(a) $\dfrac{2}{a} + \dfrac{1}{b+1}$ (b) $\dfrac{3}{x} + \dfrac{1}{x+y}$ (c) $\dfrac{x}{a} - \dfrac{x}{a+2}$

(d) $\dfrac{x}{3} + \dfrac{2}{x-1}$ (e) $\dfrac{2}{x+2} + \dfrac{3}{x-1}$ (f) $\dfrac{5}{x-3} - \dfrac{2}{x+1}$

⋆A12   A mathematician invents a new notation for writing reciprocals.
She uses $\bar{a}$ to mean $\dfrac{1}{a}$.

So, for example, $a\bar{b}$ means $a \times \dfrac{1}{b}$ or $\dfrac{a}{b}$;

$(a+b)\overline{c+d}$ means $(a+b) \times \dfrac{1}{c+d}$ or $\dfrac{a+b}{c+d}$.

(a) Write these in ordinary notation.

    (i) $ab\bar{c}$ (ii) $a\overline{bc}$ (iii) $(p+q)\bar{r}$ (iv) $p + q\bar{r}$ (v) $\overline{p+\bar{q}}$

One advantage of this new notation is that fractions can be printed on one line only.

(b) Write these in the new notation, using one line only for each one.

    (i) $\dfrac{1}{xy}$ (ii) $\dfrac{x}{y+z}$ (iii) $\dfrac{x}{z} + y$ (iv) $\dfrac{a}{b} + \dfrac{c}{d}$ (v) $\dfrac{a+b}{c}$.

(c) Which of these equations are true for **all** values of a, b and c?

    (i) $\overline{ab} = \bar{a}\bar{b}$ (ii) $\overline{a+b} = \bar{a} + \bar{b}$ (iii) $(a+b)\bar{c} = a\bar{c} + b\bar{c}$

    (iv) $a(\bar{b}+\bar{c}) = a\bar{b} + a\bar{c}$ (v) $a\,\overline{b+c} = a\bar{b} + a\bar{c}$ (iv) $\bar{\bar{a}} = a$

23

B Equations involving algebraic fractions

Worked example

Solve the equations   (a) $\dfrac{x+8}{5} = x$ (b) $\dfrac{x+3}{5} = \dfrac{x}{4}$

(a) To get rid of the '÷5' on the left-hand side, we multiply both sides by 5.

$$\text{So}\quad x + 8 = 5x$$
$$8 = 4x$$
$$2 = x$$

(b) We can get rid of the '÷5' on the left and the '÷4' on the right by multiplying both sides by 20.

$$\frac{20(x+3)}{5} = \frac{20x}{4}$$

$$\frac{4 \; \cancel{20}(x+3)}{\cancel{5}} = \frac{5 \; \cancel{20}x}{\cancel{4}}$$

$$4(x+3) = 5x$$
$$4x + 12 = 5x$$
$$12 = x$$

B1 Solve each of these equations.

(a) $\dfrac{x}{2} = x - 3$ (b) $\dfrac{x+1}{3} = x$ (c) $\dfrac{x-4}{5} = x$

B2 Solve each of these equations.

(a) $\dfrac{x+2}{3} = \dfrac{x}{2}$ (b) $\dfrac{x-3}{5} = \dfrac{x}{2}$ (c) $\dfrac{x-2}{5} = \dfrac{x+1}{2}$

Worked example

Solve the equation $\dfrac{2}{x} = \dfrac{3}{x-5}$.

First method	**Second method**
Multiply both sides by x and by $x - 5$. In other words, multiply both sides by $x(x-5)$.	Take the reciprocal of both sides.
$$\frac{2\cancel{x}(x-5)}{\cancel{x}} = \frac{3x\cancel{(x-5)}}{\cancel{x-5}}$$	$$\frac{x}{2} = \frac{x-5}{3}$$
$$2(x-5) = 3x$$	Now multiply both sides by 6, and so on.
and so on.	

B3 Solve each of these equations.

(a) $\dfrac{5}{x} = \dfrac{4}{x-2}$ (b) $\dfrac{3}{x+1} = \dfrac{7}{x}$ (c) $\dfrac{8}{x-3} = \dfrac{3}{x+1}$

C Similar triangles

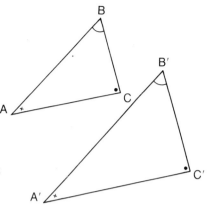

If the angles of one triangle are equal to those of
another, then the two triangles are **similar**.
Each triangle is an enlargement (or reduction) of
the other.

In the diagram on the right, ABC and A′B′C′ are
similar triangles. They have been lettered so that
the angles at A and A′ are equal, and so on.

The sides AB and A′B′ are opposite the equal angles
C and C′. We say that AB and A′B′ are
corresponding sides of the two triangles.

Suppose AB = 5 cm and A′B′ = 7 cm.
We can calculate the scale factor of the enlargement from ABC to A′B′C′
by working out $\frac{7}{5} = 1\cdot4$.

In other words, the scale factor is the ratio $\frac{A'B'}{AB}$.

We could also work out the scale factor using $\frac{B'C'}{BC}$ or $\frac{A'C'}{AC}$.

The three methods must give the same scale factor, so
$$\frac{A'B'}{AB} = \frac{B'C'}{BC} = \frac{A'C'}{AC}.$$

In problems involving similar triangles, it helps to use the letters A, B, C
and A′, B′, C′ to letter the triangles, so that the equal angles get the same
letter (either dashed or undashed).

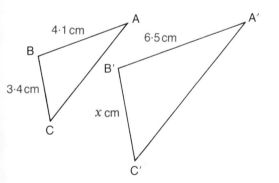

C1 If we apply the equation $\frac{A'B'}{AB} = \frac{B'C'}{BC}$
to the diagram on the left, we get
$$\frac{6\cdot5}{4\cdot1} = \frac{x}{3\cdot4}.$$

Multiply both sides by 3·4 to get
$$\frac{6\cdot5 \times 3\cdot4}{4\cdot1} = x.$$

Calculate x, to 1 d.p.

C2 Suppose in the diagram above that BC = 2·6 cm, AC = 4·7 cm,
B′C′ = 3·2 cm and A′C′ = x cm.

Calculate the value of x, to 1 d.p.

Worked example

Calculate the length marked x in this diagram.

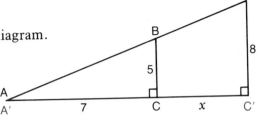

Two similar triangles have been picked out and lettered ABC and A'B'C'. (A and A' are the same point.) We use $\dfrac{A'C'}{AC} = \dfrac{B'C'}{BC}$.

$$A'C' \text{ is } 7+x, \text{ so } \quad \frac{7+x}{7} = \frac{8}{5}$$

$$\frac{7+x}{7} = 1 \cdot 6$$

Multiply both sides by 7. $\quad 7+x = 11 \cdot 2$

$$x = 4 \cdot 2$$

C3 Calculate a in the diagram on the right.

C4 Calculate x in the diagram below.

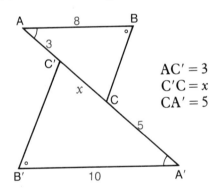

$AC' = 3$
$C'C = x$
$CA' = 5$

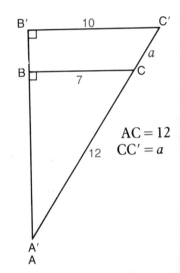

$AC = 12$
$CC' = a$

C5 (a) In the diagram on the left, which other triangle is similar to triangle DAC?

(b) Explain why $\dfrac{h}{p} = \dfrac{y}{x+y}$.

(c) Use another pair of similar triangles to write down an expression for $\dfrac{h}{q}$ in terms of x and y.

(d) Explain why $h\left(\dfrac{1}{p} + \dfrac{1}{q}\right) = 1$.

(e) Calculate h when $p = 4$ and $q = 5$.

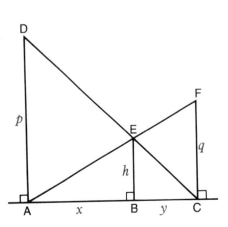

C6 The shaded part of this diagram is a rectangle 4 units by 5 units.

(a) Write down another ratio in the diagram which is equal to $\dfrac{a}{5}$.

(b) Explain why $ab = 20$.

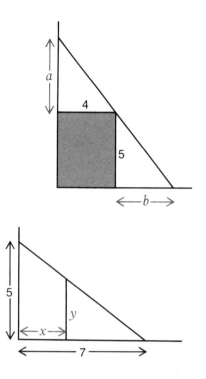

C7 Use similar triangles to get an equation connecting x and y in this diagram.

Re-write the equation so that it contains no fractions or brackets.

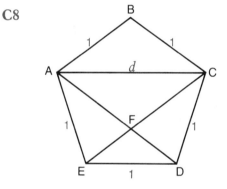

C8

ABCDE is a regular pentagon, whose sides are each 1 unit long.

Each diagonal is of length d units.

In a regular pentagon, each diagonal is parallel to one of the sides of the pentagon.

(a) What kind of shape is ABCF, and what is the length of CF?

(b) Explain why the length of EF is $d - 1$.

(c) Which triangle is similar to triangle EFD?

(d) Use the pair of similar triangles to write an equation for d, and show that the equation can be re-written as $d^2 - d - 1 = 0$.

(e) Measure the diagram to find a rough value for d. (Remember that each side is 1 unit long, and d has to be measured in the same units.)

Use the decimal search method to find d, correct to 2 decimal places.

Two special kinds of rectangle

C9 The 'A-series' of paper sizes has an interesting feature.

If you take a sheet of
one of the sizes, say A4, . . .   fold it in half, . . .   and turn it round,

then the result is the next size in the series (A5) and it is
similar to the starting rectangle.

For this to be possible the sides of the rectangle have to be in
a certain ratio.

Suppose the starting rectangle in
the diagram above has a shorter
side 1 unit long and a longer
side p units long.

(a) Write down the shorter and longer sides of the 'half-rectangle'
after it has been turned round as shown above.

(b) From the fact that the starting rectangle and the 'half-rectangle'
are similar, write down an equation for p, and solve it.

(c) Measure the sides of an A4 sheet and check that their ratio
is correct.

C10 A 'golden' rectangle has this special feature:

If you cut a square from it, . . .   the rectangle which is left is similar
to the original rectangle.

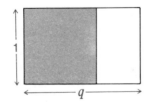

Suppose the original rectangle is 1 unit by q units.

(a) Write down the sides of the rectangle left after the square
has been removed.

(b) Write down an equation for q and solve it by decimal search.

4 Area under a graph

A Step-graph approximations to a curve

Imagine that we have a video screen and we
want to 'draw' the curve shown on the right.

We have a pen or 'plotter' which can only move
across → and up ↑ .
The distance across each time is 5 mm, but
it can be moved up any distance.

So the plotter is able to draw 'step-graphs', like
this, for example:

The plotter can draw a 'step-graph approximation' to the curve above in
two different ways.

(1) It can start by going 5 mm across, then
   up to the curve, then across again, and so on.

   This produces a step-graph which is everywhere
   below the curve (except at the points where it
   touches the curve).

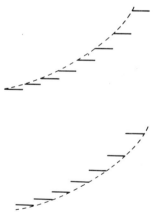

(2) Or it can start by going up, then 5 mm across
   to the curve, then up again, and so on.

   This produces a step-graph which is everywhere
   above the curve.

The curve itself is 'sandwiched' between the
'lower' and 'upper' step-graphs.

Each of the two step-graphs, the upper and the
lower, is a kind of approximation to the curve itself.
Step-graphs will become important in the work
which follows.

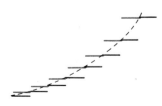

B The area under a graph

An architect has designed an exhibition hall whose roof has the shape of the graph of the function $x \rightarrow 25 - 0{\cdot}02x^2$ between $x = {}^-20$ and $x = 20$.

x is the distance in metres measured sideways from the centre line of the hall.

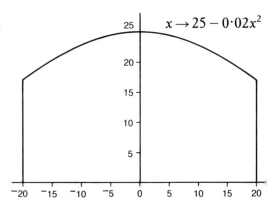

In order to design the air-conditioning system, the architect needs to know the volume of the hall. She knows its length (75 m), so she needs to find its **cross-sectional area**.

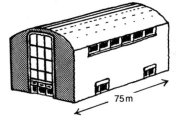

The cross-sectional area is the area under the graph of $x \rightarrow 25 - 0{\cdot}02x^2$ between $x = {}^-20$ and $x = 20$.

One way to find this area would be to plot the graph on squared paper, and count the squares under the graph.

For example, if the graph is drawn like this, each small square stands for $1\,m^2$.

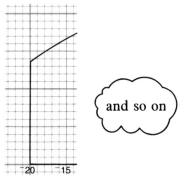

and so on

This method is time-consuming and requires accurate drawing. A method based on calculation would be better.

Here is one method which can be used.
The cross-section of the hall is symmetrical, so we need to find the area of only one half of it.

1 Split the area into vertical strips of equal width. (The width of each strip here is 5 m.)

We can use the formula $x \rightarrow 25 - 0{\cdot}02x^2$ to find the height of each of the vertical lines.

Let f stand for the function $x \rightarrow 25 - 0{\cdot}02x^2$.
Here is a table of values of f(x).

x	0	5	10	15	20
f(x)	25	24·5	23	20·5	17

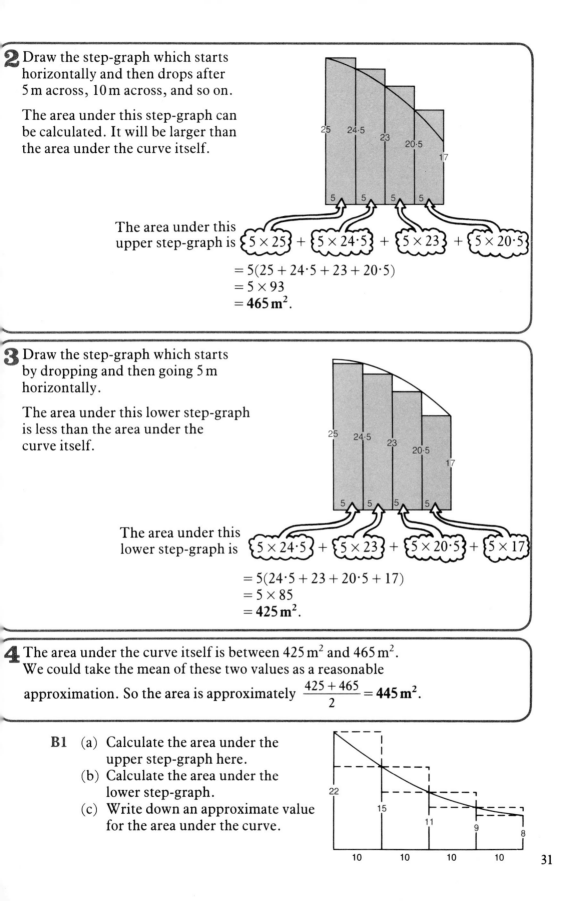

2 Draw the step-graph which starts horizontally and then drops after 5 m across, 10 m across, and so on.

The area under this step-graph can be calculated. It will be larger than the area under the curve itself.

25   24·5   23   20·5   17

5   5   5   5

The area under this upper step-graph is $\{5 \times 25\} + \{5 \times 24\cdot5\} + \{5 \times 23\} + \{5 \times 20\cdot5\}$

$$= 5(25 + 24\cdot5 + 23 + 20\cdot5)$$
$$= 5 \times 93$$
$$= \textbf{465 m}^2.$$

3 Draw the step-graph which starts by dropping and then going 5 m horizontally.

The area under this lower step-graph is less than the area under the curve itself.

25   24·5   23   20·5   17

5   5   5   5

The area under this lower step-graph is $\{5 \times 24\cdot5\} + \{5 \times 23\} + \{5 \times 20\cdot5\} + \{5 \times 17\}$

$$= 5(24\cdot5 + 23 + 20\cdot5 + 17)$$
$$= 5 \times 85$$
$$= \textbf{425 m}^2.$$

4 The area under the curve itself is between 425 m² and 465 m². We could take the mean of these two values as a reasonable approximation. So the area is approximately $\dfrac{425 + 465}{2} = \textbf{445 m}^2$.

B1 (a) Calculate the area under the upper step-graph here.
　　(b) Calculate the area under the lower step-graph.
　　(c) Write down an approximate value for the area under the curve.

22

15

11   9   8

10   10   10   10

31

B2 Use the method of upper and lower step-graphs to calculate an approximate value for the area under this curve.

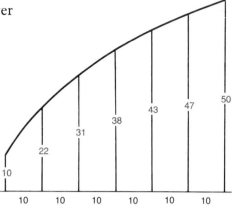

B3 The diagram below shows part of the graph of the function q, where $q(x) = 2 + 0 \cdot 1x^2$.

$$q(x) = 2 + 0 \cdot 1x^2$$

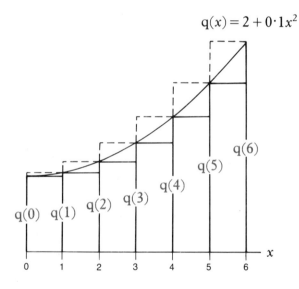

(a) Calculate the values of $q(0)$, $q(1)$, $q(2)$, . . . up to $q(6)$.

(b) Calculate the area under the upper step-graph.

(c) Calculate the area under the lower step-graph.

(d) Find an approximate value for the area under the graph of $q(x)$ between $x = 0$ and $x = 6$.

(e) Do you think your answer to part (d) is slightly greater, or slightly smaller, than the actual area under the graph? How can you tell which it is, from the shape of the graph?

We can get a better approximation to the area under a graph by using narrower strips, so that the step-graphs approximate more closely to the graph itself.

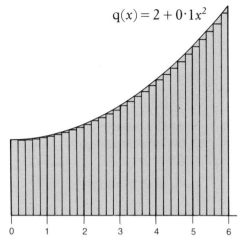

$q(x) = 2 + 0.1x^2$

The diagram on the right shows the same graph as in question B3. The strips are each of width 0.2.

Only the lower step-graph is shown. As the strips are made narrower (so that there are more and more of them), the area under the lower step-graph increases and gets closer and closer to the area under the graph itself.

Similarly the area under the upper step-graph (not shown here) decreases and gets closer and closer to the area under the graph itself.

When there are a large number of very narrow strips, the calculation of the area under the step-graph is very tedious, but simple on a computer.

This program prints out the area under the **lower** step-graph when W, the width of each strip, is 0.2.

X is used for x, Y for $q(x)$, A for the area of a strip and T for the total area so far.

To print out the area under the **upper** step-graph, replace the second line by
20   FOR X = W TO 6 STEP W

```
10 LET  W = 0·2
20 FOR  X = 0 TO 6 − W STEP W
30 LET  Y = 2 + 0·1 * X * X
40 LET  A = W * Y
50 LET  T = T + A
60 NEXT  X
70 PRINT  T
```

To get a better approximation to the area under the graph itself, reduce the width of a strip.

Here are some results obtained on a computer.

Width of strip	Area under upper step-graph	Area under lower step-graph
0·2	19·564	18·844
0·1	19·381	19·021
0·01	19·218 009 8	19·182 009 8
0·001	19·196 201 8	19·192 603
0·0001	19·200 161 9	19·199 801 9

B4   Program a computer to calculate an approximation to the area under the graph of the function $r(x) = x^3 + 1$, between $x = 0$ and $x = 5$.

33

So far all the graphs we have looked at in this chapter have sloped one way, either upwards throughout or downwards throughout.

If a graph slopes upwards in some parts and downwards in others, we can define a step-graph which approximates to the shape of the graph in the following way:

Decide on the width of strip to be used, say 0·5.

Start at a point on the graph. Go across 0·5, then **either** up **or** down (whichever it has to be) to meet the graph. Then go across 0·5 again and so on.

Here is an example.

In some places this is a lower step-graph and in others it is an upper step-graph.

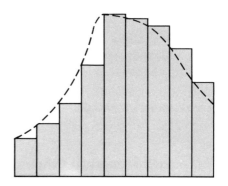

But it is still true that as the width of the strips is reduced, the area under the step-graph gets closer and closer to the area under the graph itself.

The calculation of the area under the step-graph can be carried out in the following way:

Suppose the graph is the graph of a function f(x).
Suppose x starts at a and ends at b and the width of the strips is w.

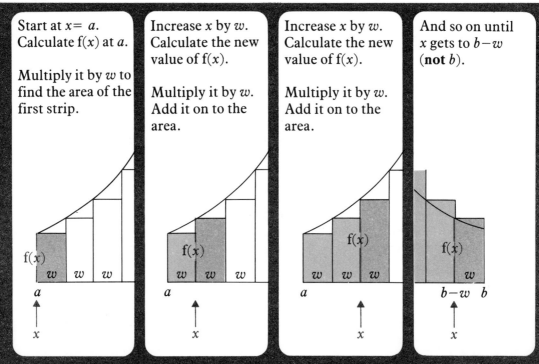

| Start at $x = a$. Calculate f(x) at a.

Multiply it by w to find the area of the first strip. | Increase x by w. Calculate the new value of f(x).

Multiply it by w. Add it on to the area. | Increase x by w. Calculate the new value of f(x).

Multiply it by w. Add it on to the area. | And so on until x gets to $b-w$ (**not** b). |

B5 This diagram shows the graph of the function $s(x) = x^2(3 - x)$.

It also shows an approximating step-graph, with strips of width 0.5.

(a) The flowchart below shows how to calculate the area under the step-graph.
Follow the instructions yourself.

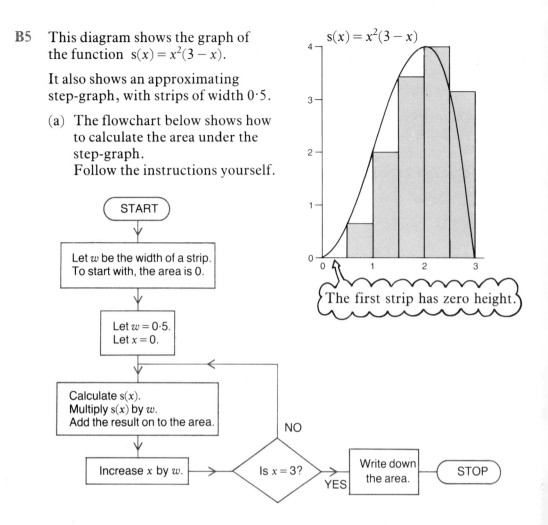

$$s(x) = x^2(3 - x)$$

The first strip has zero height.

START

Let w be the width of a strip.
To start with, the area is 0.

Let $w = 0.5$.
Let $x = 0$.

Calculate $s(x)$.
Multiply $s(x)$ by w.
Add the result on to the area.

Increase x by w. → Is $x = 3$? — NO

YES → Write down the area. → STOP

(b) Re-do the calculation with $w = 0.2$.

(It can be shown that the actual value of the area is **6·75**.)

B6 Calculate an approximation to the area under the graph of $y = x(4 - x)$ between $x = 0$ and $x = 4$, using strips of width

(a) 0.5 (b) 0.2

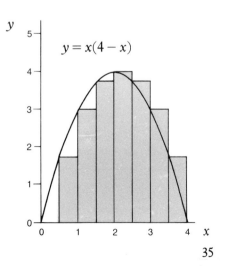

$$y = x(4 - x)$$

C   The trapezium rule

The work in this section involves calculating the areas of **trapeziums**.
A trapezium is a quadrilateral with one pair of parallel sides.

Let a and b be the lengths of the parallel sides
of a trapezium, and let h be the distance
between them (measured at right-angles to them).

The area of the trapezium is given by the formula

$$\text{Area} = \tfrac{1}{2}h(a+b).$$

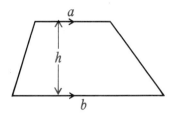

There are several different ways of explaining why this formula is correct.
Here is one way.

1 Draw a line across the
trapezium, parallel to
the parallel sides and
halfway between them.
Call its ends P and Q.

2 Rotate the top section of the trapezium through 180°
about Q. It then joins up with the bottom section to
form a parallelogram.

The base of this parallelogram is $a + b$.
The height is $\tfrac{1}{2}h$. So its area is $\tfrac{1}{2}h(a+b)$.

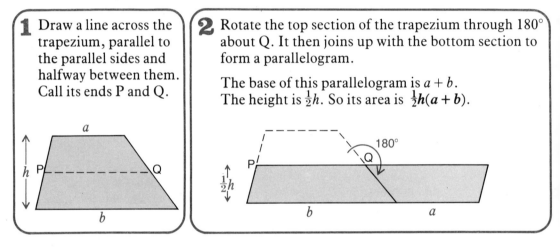

C1 Calculate the area of each of these trapeziums.

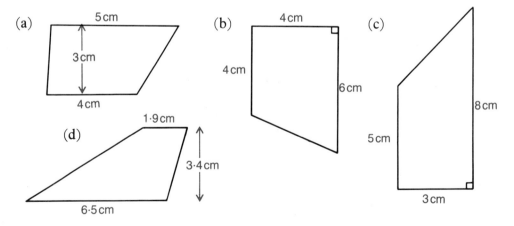

C2 What sort of 'trapezium' do you get when $a = 0$?
Does the formula for the area still work in this case?

The **trapezium rule** is another method of calculating, approximately, the area under a curve. Here is an example to explain the method.

Suppose we want to find the area under the curve shown on the right.

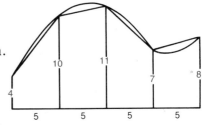

As before, we split the area into strips of equal width. Here the width of each strip is 5.

We replace the curve by a set of straight lines as shown. The area under this set of straight lines is an approximation to the area under the curve.

Each of the four shapes A, B, C and D is a trapezium. So we can use the formula $\frac{1}{2}h(a+b)$ to find the area of each one.

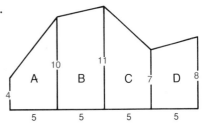

h is 5 for each trapezium.

Area A $= \frac{5}{2}(4 + 10)$

Area B $= \frac{5}{2}(10 + 11)$

Area C $= \frac{5}{2}(11 + 7)$

Area D $= \frac{5}{2}(7 + 8)$

The areas have been set out like this on purpose, so that you can see an 'overlapping' pattern. For example '10' comes into the expression for area A and for area B.

We can set out the complete calculation of the total area like this:

$\frac{5}{2}(4 + 10$
$\quad + 10 + 11$
$\quad\quad + 11 + 7$
$\quad\quad\quad + 7 + 8)$

The reason why the three 'middle' heights each occur twice in the brackets is because each is a side of two trapeziums, one on the left and one on the right.

The **trapezium rule** for an approximation to the area under a graph is

$$\frac{\text{Width of strip}}{2} \times (\text{1st height} + 2 \times \text{each intermediate height} + \text{last height})$$

The result for the curve above is $\frac{5}{2}(4 + 2 \times 10 + 2 \times 11 + 2 \times 7 + 8) = \mathbf{170}$.

C3 Use the trapezium rule to find an approximation to the area under the curve on the right.

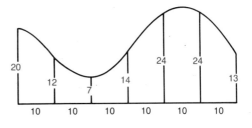

C4 A metalworker has designed a scoop.

The curved part of the scoop is made from a piece of sheet metal whose shape is shown in the diagram below, which is $\frac{1}{2}$ **full size**.

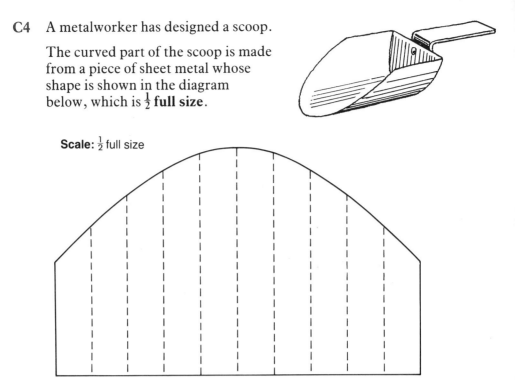

Scale: $\frac{1}{2}$ full size

Take measurements from the drawing and calculate an approximation to the area of the piece of metal, using the trapezium rule.
Remember that the scale of the drawing is $\frac{1}{2}$ full size.

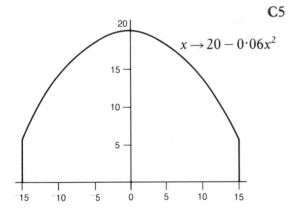

$x \rightarrow 20 - 0{\cdot}06x^2$

C5 The roof of an aircraft hangar has the shape of the graph of $x \rightarrow 20 - 0{\cdot}06x^2$ between $x = {}^-15$ and $x = 15$.

(Measurements are in metres.)

(a) Calculate the height of the roof at $x = 0$, $x = 5$, $x = 10$ and $x = 15$.

(b) Use the trapezium rule to find an approximation to the cross-sectional area of the hangar.

(c) The hangar is 150 m long. Calculate its volume, approximately.

C6 (a) At what values of x does the graph of $x \rightarrow (x-1)(5-x)$ cross the x-axis?
(b) Sketch the shape of the graph between these two points.
(c) Use the trapezium rule with strips of width $0{\cdot}5$ to calculate an approximation to the area under the graph between the two points where it crosses the x-axis.
(d) Is your approximate value too large or too small? How can you tell?

D   Area under a graph of (time, speed)

A car travels at a constant speed of 4 m/s
for 6 seconds.

The graph on the right is a (time, speed)
graph for the car. It shows that the speed
stayed constant at 4 m/s during the
6 seconds.

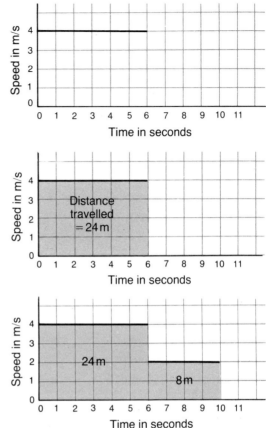

During the 6 seconds the car, going at
4 m/s, travelled a distance of 24 metres.

This distance, 24 m, is represented in the
graph by the **area** under the graph,
which is the area of a rectangle 4 by 6.

Suppose the car's speed suddenly drops to
2 m/s, and the car goes on at 2 m/s for
4 seconds.

The extra distance, 8 m, is represented
by the extra area under the graph.

(Of course, a sudden drop in speed like this
is not physically possible.)

D1   Calculate the distance travelled by each of the cars whose
(time, speed) graphs are shown below.

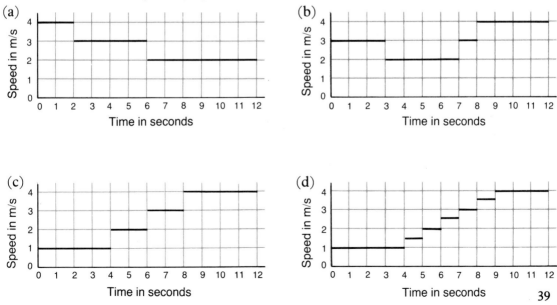

(a)

(b)

(c)

(d)

The car shown in this graph goes at 1 m/s for 1 second.

Then it goes a little faster for 1 second.

Then it goes a little faster for 1 more second, and so on.

After 8 seconds, its speed has reached 5 m/s.

The shaded area under the graph shows the distance travelled in the 8 seconds.

In this graph, the car increases its speed after every $\frac{1}{2}$ second between 0 and 8 seconds.

The shaded area shows the distance it travels in the 8 seconds.

Imagine that the 'steps' in the graph get shorter and shorter.

The graph becomes a continuous curve which shows the car's speed increasing gradually between 0 and 8 seconds.

The area under the graph shows the distance travelled.

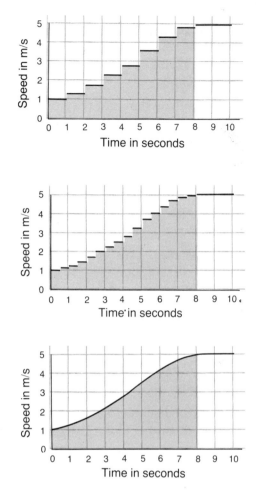

> Distance travelled = Area under (time, speed) graph

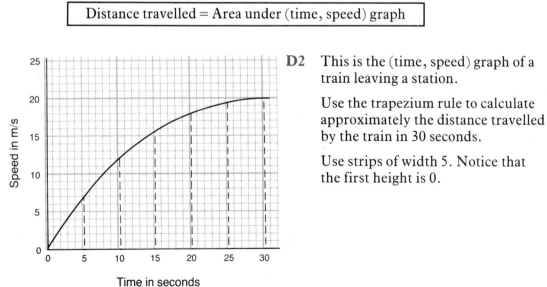

D2 This is the (time, speed) graph of a train leaving a station.

Use the trapezium rule to calculate approximately the distance travelled by the train in 30 seconds.

Use strips of width 5. Notice that the first height is 0.

40

D3 A train is travelling at 30 m/s when the brakes are applied. t seconds after applying the brakes the speed of the train is $30 - 0 \cdot 3t^2$ m/s. The (time, speed) graph looks like this.

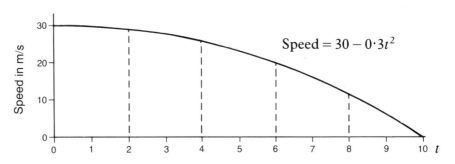

Calculate the speed at 2-second intervals and use the trapezium rule to calculate approximately the distance travelled by the train during braking.

If the vertical axis shows the rate of flow of water in litres per second, and the horizontal axis shows time in seconds, then the area under the graph represents the amount of water in litres which flows in a given period of time.

D4 The rate of flow of water from a hosepipe varied during a period of 60 seconds as shown in the graph below.

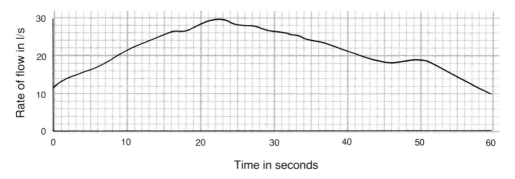

Use the trapezium rule with strips of width 10 to calculate approximately the volume of water which flowed from the hosepipe during the 60 seconds.

D5 The rate of flow of water, r litre/min, from a tank is given by the formula $r = 10 \times 2^{-t}$, where t is the time in minutes from when the tap is opened.

(a) Calculate r when t is 0, 1, 2, 3, 4 and 5.

(b) Use the trapezium rule to estimate the volume of water which flows from the tank in the first five minutes.

41

Money matters: VAT

The things which people spend their money on can be divided up
into **goods** and **services**.

'Goods' are the things you buy from shops or mail order firms, such as food, clothes, records, computers, and so on.	'Services' are things that other people do for you, such as repair your bike or TV set.

VAT is a tax which is charged on most goods and services.
The tax goes to the government to help pay the cost of running the
country.

For some goods you do not have to pay VAT.
Examples are books and take away cold foods.

DUMPLINGS PRICE LIST

	Eat here	Take out
Plain	80p	70p
Beef	£1·03	90p
Apple	86p	75p
Banana	92p	80p

The rate of VAT is fixed by the government. The rate may be
changed from time to time. If there is a change, it is usually
announced in an annual Budget in March.

Suppose the rate of VAT is 15%. You want to buy a bike whose
price excluding VAT is £80.
If you buy the bike you will be charged £80 + 15% of £80 = £80 + £12 = **£92**.

    1   Find out the present rate of VAT. Work out the cost,
          including VAT, of an item whose price excluding VAT is

          (a) £10   (b) £20   (c) £50   (d) £55   (e) £58·50

Suppose you are in business. You buy materials, from which you make things to sell to other people.

You pay VAT when you buy the materials, but **you get this back from the taxman**.

What happens is illustrated in this story.

The story: Alan sells Brenda the wood to make a dog kennel.
Brenda makes the kennel, and sells it to Colin, who paints it.
Diana buys the kennel from Colin.

The rate of VAT at the time is 10%.

Brenda buys the wood from Alan.
Alan charges £20 + VAT = £**22**.

Alan keeps £20.
He pays £2 VAT to the taxman.

Colin buys the kennel from Brenda.
Brenda charges £60 +VAT = £**66**.

Brenda keeps £60.
She pays the £6 VAT to the taxman.
She gets back the £2 VAT she paid on the wood.

Diana buys the kennel from Colin.
Colin charges £100 + VAT = £**110**

Colin keeps £100.
He pays the £10 VAT to the taxman.
He gets back the £6 VAT he paid on the kennel.

At each stage the taxman collects 10% of the **value added** to the kennel.
For example, Colin buys it for £60 and sells it for £100.
The value added is £40, so the taxman gets £4 from Colin. (Colin gives him £10 but gets £6 back.)

At the end of the story, the taxman has made a gain of £10, which is 10% of the final selling price of the kennel.

1 Surfaces

1.1 This diagram shows the curved surface of a
cylinder, of radius 5 cm and height 10 cm.

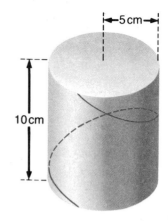

(a) Calculate the area of the curved surface.

(b) The helix goes once round the cylinder.
Calculate its length.

(c) Calculate the angle which the helix
makes with the base of the cylinder.

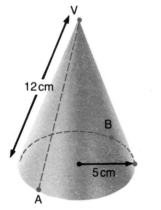

1.2 The cone shown here is cut along the line AV and
flattened out.

(a) Sketch the flattened-out shape.

(b) Calculate the angle of the sector.

(c) The point B is diametrically opposite A.
Draw the sector to scale and measure the
shortest distance on the cone from A to B.

1.3 This diagram shows a cube whose edges
are 5 cm long.
The point B is at the centre of a face.

Calculate the shortest distance from
A to B on the surface of the cube.

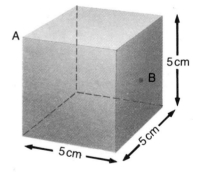

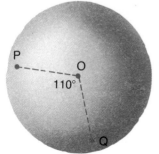

1.4 P and Q are two points on the surface of a sphere of
radius 5 cm. O is the centre of the sphere and the
angle POQ is 110°.

Calculate the length of the shortest path on the sphere
from P to Q.

2 Optimisation

2.1 A plumber has copper pipes in standard lengths of 200 cm.
She needs pieces of these lengths (in cm):

130   110   100   75   75   70   70   65   60   50   45

(a) Her first priority is to use as few standard lengths as possible.
What is the smallest number she will need?

(b) When she cuts the standard lengths up, there will be some waste.
The waste is more useful if it is in a few long pieces than in a
lot of short pieces. So her second priority is to achieve this.
Find the best way of cutting the standard lengths.

2.2 A truck can carry up to 1000 kg.
Cookers weigh 200 kg and are worth £140. Fridges weigh 160 kg and
are worth £120. Washing machines weigh 300 kg and are worth £200.

What is the most valuable load the truck can carry?

3 Algebraic fractions

3.1 Express each of these as the sum or difference of two fractions,
and simplify the fractions where possible.

(a) $\dfrac{3a + 12b}{4}$ (b) $\dfrac{a^2 + b^2}{ab}$ (c) $\dfrac{3x - 2y}{xy}$ (d) $\dfrac{3a - 2a^2}{a^2}$

3.2 Express each of these as a single fraction.

(a) $\dfrac{2}{x} + \dfrac{3}{y}$ (b) $\dfrac{3}{x} + \dfrac{1}{x^2}$ (c) $\dfrac{3}{ax} - \dfrac{2}{bx}$ (d) $\dfrac{a}{p} + \dfrac{b}{pq}$

(e) $\dfrac{3}{x} + \dfrac{2}{x + 1}$ (f) $\dfrac{4}{x} - \dfrac{3}{x - 1}$ (g) $\dfrac{3}{a} + \dfrac{2}{b + 1}$ (h) $\dfrac{4}{x - 2} - \dfrac{2}{x + 3}$

3.3 Solve each of these equations.

(a) $\dfrac{x}{7 \cdot 3} = \dfrac{4 \cdot 2}{1 \cdot 6}$ (b) $\dfrac{5 \cdot 3}{x} = \dfrac{0 \cdot 5}{2 \cdot 6}$ (c) $\dfrac{x + 3}{3} = \dfrac{5}{4}$ (d) $\dfrac{2}{5} = \dfrac{7}{x + 2}$

3.4 Calculate the length marked x in
this diagram.

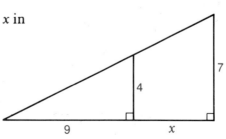

45

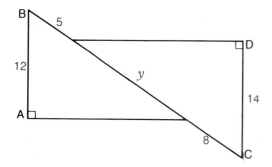

3.5 Calculate the length marked y in this diagram.
(AB is parallel to CD.)

4 Area under a graph

4.1 This is part of the graph of the function $r(x) = \dfrac{1}{x}$.

(a) Calculate the area under the upper step-graph.

(b) Calculate the area under the lower step-graph.

(c) State a reasonable approximation for the area under the curve.

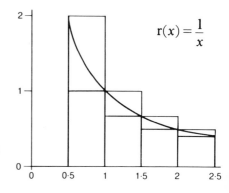

4.2 The diagram below shows the cross-section of a river.
Use the trapezium rule to estimate the area of the cross-section.

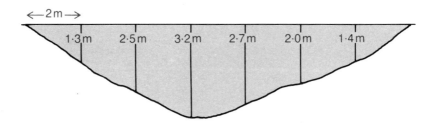

4.3 At a protest march, an observer is estimating the number of people taking part. She counts the number of people who pass her in 1 minute, and does this once every 15 minutes. The march starts at 11 a.m. Here are her results.

Time	11:00	11:15	11:30	11:45	12:00	12:15	12:30	12:45
Rate of passing, in people per minute	120	150	180	190	200	180	140	70

Draw a graph and estimate the total number of people on the march.

5 The sine and cosine functions (1)

A Sine and cosine: a reminder

Here are reminders of the two basic formulas involving sine and cosine
and the sides of a right-angled triangle.

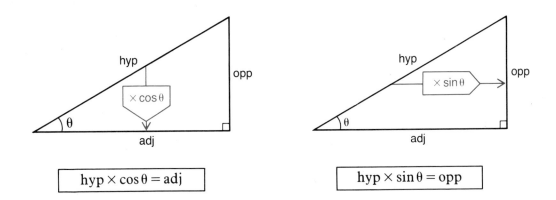

$$\boxed{\text{hyp} \times \cos \theta = \text{adj}}$$ $$\boxed{\text{hyp} \times \sin \theta = \text{opp}}$$

A1 Calculate the sides marked with letters in each of
these right-angled triangles.

Give each length to the nearest $0 \cdot 1$ cm.

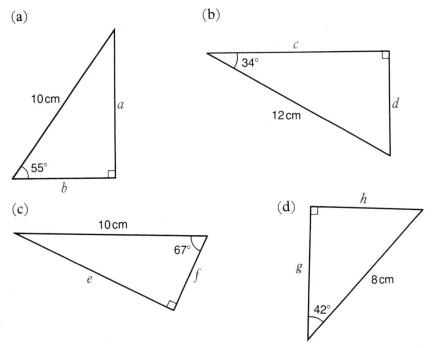

47

B The unit circle

Although cosine and sine were introduced in connection with right-angled triangles, they also have a close relationship with the **circle**, as we shall now see.

This diagram shows the circle whose centre O is at $(0, 0)$ and whose radius is 1 unit. We call it the **unit circle**.

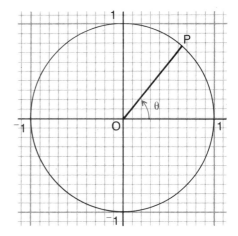

Let P be a point on the unit circle. If we want to tell someone exactly where P is, we can give the angle between the positive x-axis and OP.

We shall call this angle θ, and we will always measure it **anticlockwise**, starting from the positive x-axis.

Another way to state the position of P is to give the **coordinates** of P.

If we know the angle θ, we can work out the coordinates of P.

Suppose θ is $50°$.

We can use the right-angled triangle shown in this diagram to find the coordinates of P.

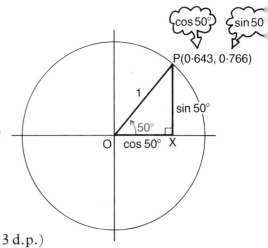

The x-coordinate of P is the side OX which is adjacent to $50°$.
So the x-coordinate of $P = \text{hyp} \times \cos 50°$
$$= 1 \ \times \cos 50°$$
$$= \mathbf{\cos 50°}$$

From a calculator, $\cos 50° = 0{\cdot}643$ (to 3 d.p.) and this is the x-coordinate of P.

The y-coordinate of P is the side XP which is opposite $50°$.
So the y-coordinate of $P = \text{hyp} \times \sin 50°$
$$= 1 \ \times \sin 50°$$
$$= \mathbf{\sin 50°} = 0{\cdot}766 \text{ (to 3 d.p.)}$$

B1 Draw a unit circle to a large scale (say 5 cm to 1 unit) on graph paper. Mark the point P for which the angle θ is $35°$.

(a) Use a calculator to find the coordinates of P and check from your diagram.

(b) Do the same for $\theta = 75°$. Keep the diagram for later.

48

The circle is divided by the x- and y-axes into four **quadrants**, which are usually numbered anticlockwise as shown here.

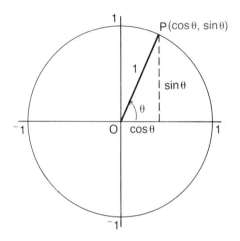

So far we have been looking at points on the unit circle which are in the **first quadrant**.

We have found that if the line OP makes an angle θ with the x-axis, then

the x-coordinate of P is **cos θ**,
the y -coordinate of P is **sin θ**.

If the angle θ is greater than 90°, then P will be in the 2nd, 3rd or 4th quadrants. We have not yet given any meaning to sines and cosines of angles greater than 90°.
This is because we have used sines and cosines in connection with right-angled triangles, and none of the angles in a right-angled triangle can be more than 90°.

But the unit circle diagram can be used to give meaning to cosines and sines of angles of any size.

We simply say that for **any** angle θ,

cos θ = the x-coordinate of P,   sin θ = the y-coordinate of P.

For example, when θ = 130°, we find from a calculator that cos 130° = ⁻0·643 (to 3 d.p.)
and sin 130° = 0·766 (to 3 d.p.)

(⁻0·643 , 0·766) are the coordinates of P when the angle θ is 130°.

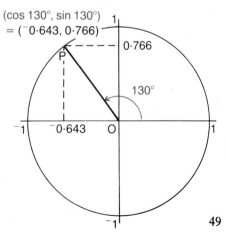

B2 On the diagram for question B1 mark P so that the angle θ is 160°.

Use a calculator to find cos 160° and sin 160° and check that these are the coordinates of P on the diagram.

49

C The sine function

The sine of θ is the *y*-coordinate of the point P
on the unit circle.

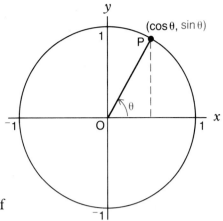

We shall see what happens to sin θ as θ increases
from 0° to 360°.

The diagram below shows the values (to 2 d.p.) of
cos θ and sin θ for angles from 0° to 360° in
steps of 15°.

cos θ is shown in black and sin θ in red.

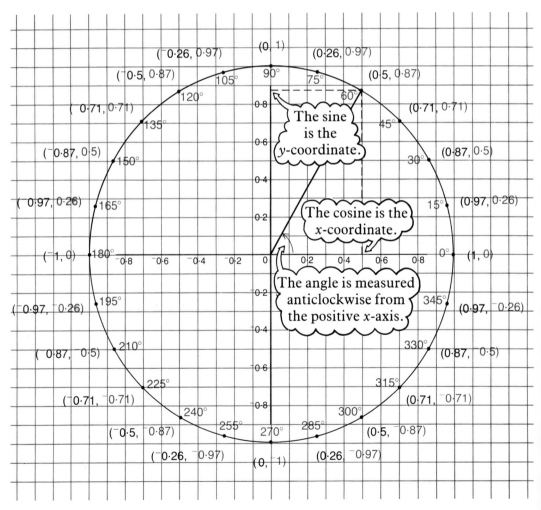

We shall start by looking at the values of sin θ only.

When θ is 0°, sin θ is 0.
As θ goes from 0° to 15°, sin θ increases by 0·26.

As θ goes from 15° to 30°, from 30° to 45°, and so on, sin θ increases
by less and less each time.
Between θ = 75° and θ = 90°, sin θ increases by only 0·03.

This is because of the shape of the circle. The *y*-coordinate of P
goes up by less and less as P gets towards the top of the circle.

Here is the start of the graph of the function θ → sin θ.

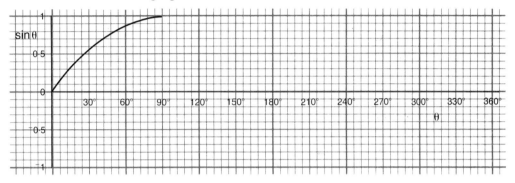

Between θ = 90° and θ = 180°, sin θ decreases from 1 down to 0, slowly at
first and then faster.
The graph continues like this.

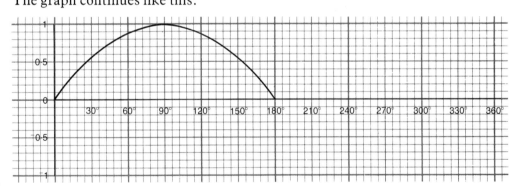

C1 (a) Copy this graph, preferably to a larger scale, and complete it
to show the function θ → sin θ for values of θ from 0° to 360°.

(b) Draw a sketch to show how the graph continues beyond θ = 360°.

C2 Draw a graph of the function θ → cos θ for values of θ from
0° to 360°.

51

The functions $\theta \rightarrow \sin \theta$ and $\theta \rightarrow \cos \theta$ are **periodic functions**.
Their graphs 'repeat themselves' after every 360°.
We say 360° is the **period** of each of the functions.

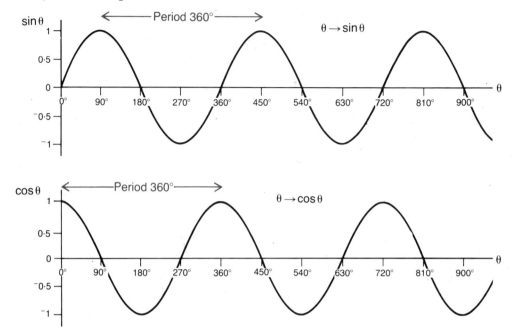

The graph of $\theta \rightarrow \cos \theta$ has the same overall shape as the graph of $\theta \rightarrow \sin \theta$, but it is shifted 90° to the left.

D Inverse sine

If we use a calculator to find $\sin 30°$, we get $\sin 30° = 0.5$.
0.5 is the sine of 30°, and 30° is the **inverse sine** of 0.5.

We write this $\text{inv} \sin 0.5 = 30°$.

If we enter 0.5 on the calculator and press $\boxed{\text{inv}}$ $\boxed{\text{sin}}$ (or its equivalent) we get 30.

But 30° is not the only angle whose sine is 0.5.

In the range 0° to 360° there are **two** angles whose sines are 0.5.

They are 30° and 150°, as you can see from this diagram.

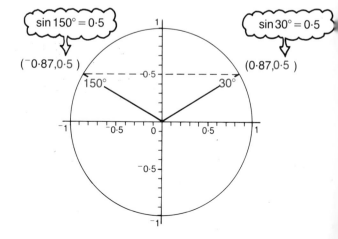

52

You can also see this from the graph of $\theta \to \sin\theta$.

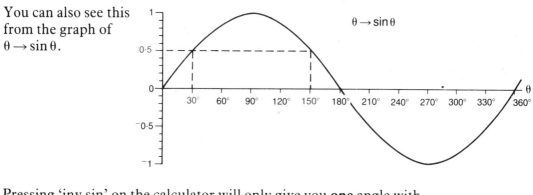

Pressing 'inv sin' on the calculator will only give you **one** angle with a given sine. To find the other, you have to think about the circle diagram (or the graph).

The two angles with the same sine are symmetrically placed either side of 90°.

So, for example, if one angle is 75°, the other must be 105°, as you can see from this diagram. Check on a calculator that $\sin 105° = \sin 75°$.

D1 Which other angle in the range 0° to 360° has the same sine as each of these angles? (Sketch a circle diagram to help, if you like.)

(a) 40° (b) 10° (c) 115° (d) 29° (e) 53·2° (f) 106·1°

Check each answer by finding sines on a calculator.

D2 (a) Use a calculator to find inv sin 0·3 to the nearest degree.

(b) Write down, to the nearest degree, the other angle in the range 0° to 360° whose sine is also 0·3.

(c) Check on the calculator that the sine of this other angle is the same as that of the first angle.

D3 For each of these equations, find **two** values of θ in the range 0° to 360°. Give each angle to the nearest degree.

(a) $\sin\theta = 0·63$ (b) $\sin\theta = 0·754$ (c) $\sin\theta = 0·209$

D4 Answer this question without looking at any of the diagrams on this page or the opposite page. (Cover them up.)

(a) Which angle in the range 0° to 360° has the same sine as
(i) 37° (ii) 129° (iii) 8° (iv) 52·6°

(b) Find two values of θ in the range 0° to 360° for which $\sin\theta = 0·313$.

53

Suppose you want to know the angles (in the range 0° to 360°) whose sines are both ⁻0·5.

If you use a calculator to find inv sin ⁻0·5, the result will be ⁻**30°**.

⁻30° means 30° measured **clockwise** from 0°. So ⁻30° is equivalent to **330°** anticlockwise.

The other angle whose sine is also ⁻0·5 can be found from the circle diagram. It is **210°**.

Check on a calculator that
$$\sin 210° = \sin 330° = \sin(⁻30°).$$

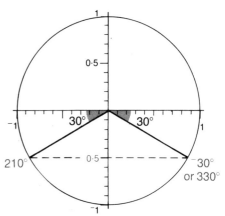

D5 (a) Use a calculator to find inv sin ⁻0·56, to the nearest degree. (The result will be negative.)

(b) Write down, to the nearest degree, two angles in the range 0° to 360° whose sines are both ⁻0·56.

D6 Find two values of θ in the range 0° to 360° for which sin θ = ⁻0·78. Give each angle correct to the nearest degree.

D7 For each of these equations, find two values of θ in the range 0° to 360°. Give each angle correct to the nearest degree.

(a) sin θ = ⁻0·29 (b) sin θ = 0·45 (c) sin θ = ⁻0·1

(d) sin θ = 0·1 (e) sin θ = ⁻0·9 (f) sin θ = 0·68

E Inverse cosine

There are two angles in the range 0° to 360° whose cosines are 0·5.

They are 60° and 300°.

This time the two angles are symmetrically placed either side of 0°. (300° is equivalent to ⁻60°.)

If you use a calculator to find inv cos 0·5 you will get the single result 60°. To get the other angle you have to think about the circle diagram.

Check on a calculator that cos 300° = cos 60°.

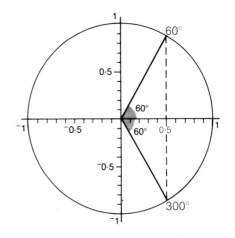

The two angles whose cosines are 0·5 can also be seen from the graph of θ → cos θ.

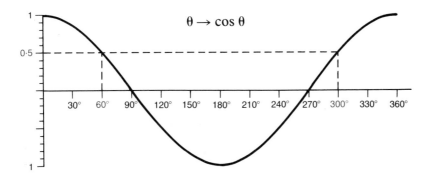

E1 Which other angle in the range 0° to 360° has the same cosine as each of these angles? (Sketch a circle diagram to help, if you like.)

(a) 50° (b) 45° (c) 130° (d) 115° (e) 240° (f) 340°

Check each answer by finding the cosines on a calculator.

E2 (a) Use a calculator to find inv cos 0·8, to the nearest degree.

(b) Write down, to the nearest degree, the other angle in the range 0° to 360° whose cosine is also 0·8.

(c) Check on a calculator that the cosine of this other angle is the same as that of the first angle.

E3 For each of these equations, find two values of θ in the range 0° to 360°. Give each angle to the nearest degree.

(a) cos θ = 0·71 (b) cos θ = 0·326 (c) cos θ = 0·404

E4 (a) Which other angle in the range 0° to 360° has the same cosine as 145°? Sketch a circle diagram to help, if you like.

(b) Check on a calculator that the cosines of the two angles are equal.

E5 For each of these equations, find two values of θ in the range 0° to 360°. Give each angle to the nearest degree.

(a) cos θ = ⁻0·5 (b) cos θ = ⁻0·6 (c) cos θ = ⁻0·138

E6 For each equation below, find two values of θ in the range 0° to 360°. Give each angle to the nearest degree.

(a) sin θ = 0·625 (b) sin θ = ⁻0·833 (c) cos θ = 0·213

(d) cos θ = ⁻0·375 (e) sin θ = 0·208 (f) cos θ = 0·333

Money matters: Insurance

Holiday medical insurance

If you go abroad for a holiday, you may
fall ill or have an accident, and need
medical treatment.

Medical treatment is often expensive
abroad.

So it is a good idea to **insure** yourself
against medical expenses.

To do this, you pay a fairly small amount of money, called a **premium**,
to an insurance company. The company then agrees to pay any
medical expenses which may arise on your holiday, up to a certain amount.

Here for example are the premiums
charged by the 'Globule Insurance Co.'
for different lengths of holiday.

Globule Insurance		10 days	20 days	30 days
Medical	£1000	£1·50	£2·75	£4·00
expenses	£5000	£5·00	£8·50	£11·50
up to	£10000	£8·00	£14·50	£19·50

Why is the insurance company willing to do this? They know,
from past experience, that most holidaymakers do not fall ill or
have accidents on holiday. So most of the people who pay their
premiums will not need to have medical expenses paid for them.

The company tries to fix the premiums so that it can pay the expenses
of the few people who do need treatment out of the total of all the
premiums paid in. It also makes sure that there is enough left over
to pay the costs of running the business, and make a profit.

Insurance companies know from experience that in some parts of the
world a holidaymaker is more likely to need medical treatment than
in others. So the premiums for these places are higher.

1 Insurance companies generally have higher premiums for
   winter sports holidays than for summer holidays. Why is this?

Car and motorcycle insurance

Motorcyclists and car drivers are required by law to be insured.
There are three main types of insurance they can have.

(1) **Third party.** If the driver (or rider) is involved in an accident in which another person is injured or killed or another vehicle damaged, the insurance company pays any compensation, and the cost of any repairs to the other vehicle.

(2) **Third party, fire and theft.** The insurance company also pays if the driver's own vehicle is damaged by fire or stolen.

(3) **Comprehensive.** The company also pays for the repairs to the driver's own vehicle if it is damaged in an accident.

The premium which the driver pays depends on a number of things:
the type of insurance; the driver's age and occupation; where the driver lives;
the make, model and age of the car or motorbike.

Different companies have different premiums, so it is a good idea to
shop around to get the best deal.

The premium covers one year's insurance. If the insurance company does
not have to pay out anything during that year, then it usually gives the
driver a **no claims discount** on his or her next year's premium.
Here is an example of the 'no claims discounts' offered by one company.

1 year's claim-free insurance	25% discount	This means the driver pays 25% less than the normal premium.
2 years' claim-free insurance	40% discount	
3 years' claim-free insurance	50% discount	
4 or more years' claim-free insurance	60% discount	

If the company has to pay out during a year's insurance, the driver
loses two years' discount. (So 60% discount becomes 40%, 50% becomes 25%.)

2   Janice is 22 years old, lives in Birmingham and drives an
8 year old Ford Escort 1300.

In her first year of driving she was comprehensively insured
and paid the normal premium of £180.

She is a very careful driver, and she made no claim during that
year (so the insurance company did not have to pay out anything).
So she was allowed a 25% no claims discount on her premium for
the second year.

(a) If the normal premium was still £180, what did Janice have to
pay in her second year?

(b) Janice made no claim during her second year and she is now
going to insure for her third year. The insurance company allows
her a 40% no claims discount. The company has increased all
its premiums, so the normal premium is now £210.
What will Janice have to pay?

6 The Earth

A Great circles

The Earth is very nearly a sphere, whose radius[1] is approximately 6400 km.

Although the surface of the Earth is 'bumpy' because of mountains and ocean depths, the bumps and dips are tiny in relation to the overall size of the Earth.

If the Earth were reduced to about the size of a football, the highest mountain (Mount Everest) would be a bump about 0·2 mm high, and the deepest part of the ocean would be a dip about 0·2 mm deep.

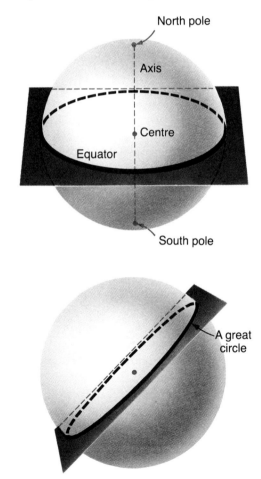

The **axis** of the Earth is the line joining the north and south poles and going through the centre of the Earth.

The Earth rotates about the axis.

The plane which goes through the Earth's centre and is at right-angles to the axis divides the Earth into two **hemispheres** (half-spheres). These are the northern and southern hemispheres.

The circular boundary where the two hemispheres meet is the **equator**.

The equator is one example of a **great circle**.

Any plane through the Earth's centre cuts the Earth's surface in a great circle.

A great circle divides the Earth into two hemispheres.

The centre of a great circle is at the Earth's centre, and its radius is the radius of the Earth itself.

---

[1] In fact the distance from the centre of the Earth to one of the poles is slightly less than the distance to points on the equator.

Great circles are very important in navigation, because the shortest path between two points on the Earth's surface is along the great circle which goes through the two points.

This diagram shows the shortest path between London and San Francisco (USA).

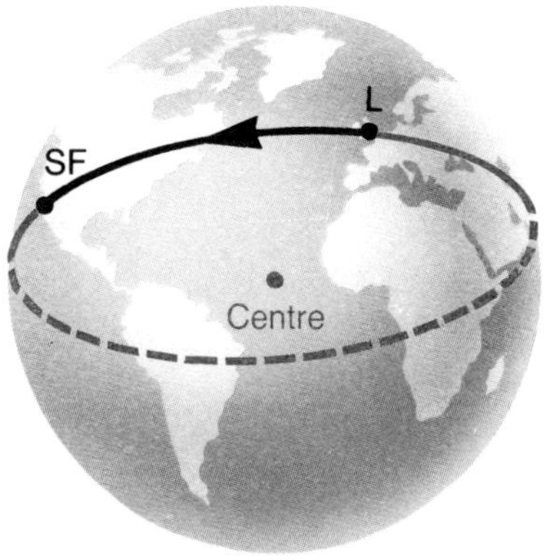

This diagram shows a great circle which goes through both poles.

Each half of the circle (from pole to pole) is called a **meridian**.

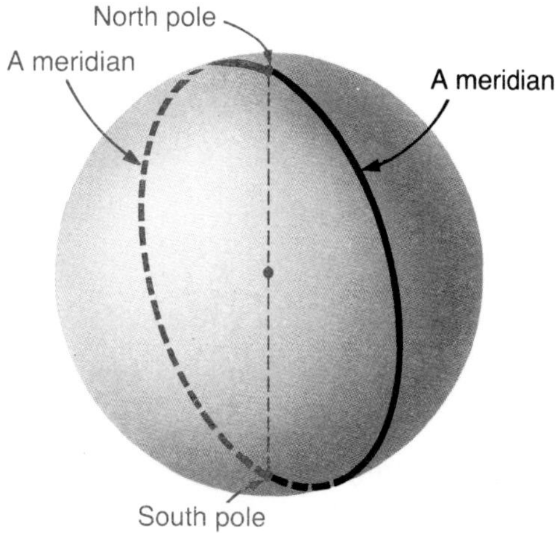

A1 The radius of the Earth is approximately 6400 km. Calculate the length of the equator.

A2 Calculate the length of a meridian.

A3 An aircraft flies from a point on the equator to the north pole by the shortest route. How far does it travel?

A4 The metre as a unit of length was first introduced by the French during the rule of Napoleon.
It was defined as a certain fraction of half of a meridian (based on the best estimates at the time of the length of a meridian).

What fraction of half a meridian do you think it was?

A5 Suppose P is a point on the Earth's surface. If a straight line is drawn from P through the Earth's centre it will meet the surface again at a point P′. P′ is called the **antipode** of P.

What is the shortest distance on the Earth's surface from a point to its antipode?

B Latitude

Latitude and longitude together are a method of stating the position of a point on the Earth's surface. They are both **angles**, and are measured in degrees.

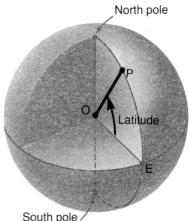

Let P be a point on the Earth's surface.

Suppose the meridian through P crosses the equator at the point E.

Let O be the centre of the Earth.

The angle EOP is called the **latitude** of P.

The latitude can be measured northwards or southwards.

In this diagram,

the latitude of Q is **60°N**,

the latitude of R is **15°S**.

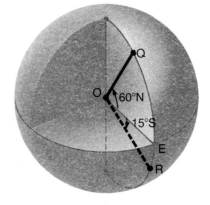

B1 (a) Which point on the Earth's surface has latitude 90°N?

(b) What is the latitude of the south pole?

(c) Which points have latitude 0° (N or S)?

B2 Calculate the distance along the meridian from E to Q in the second diagram above.

(**Hint.** What fraction of a great circle is it? Remember that each meridian is itself half of a great circle.)

B3 (a) Calculate the distance from E to R along the meridian.

(b) Calculate the distance from R to Q along the meridian.

In this diagram, the points Q and S have the same latitude, 60°N.

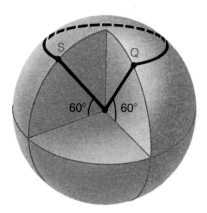

All the points on the Earth's surface whose latitude is 60°N lie on a circle.

This circle is called the **60°N circle of latitude**, or the **60°N parallel of latitude**.

The diagram below shows circles of latitude in the northern hemisphere. (A similar diagram can be drawn for the southern hemisphere.)

The latitudes 0°, 10°, 20°, . . . are shown.
The points where these circles cut a meridian are equally spaced along the meridian.

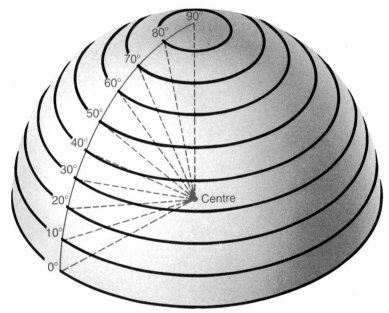

B4 Which of the places in the list below is
(a) closest to the north pole   (b) closest to the south pole
(c) closest to the equator

Place	Latitude	Place	Latitude
London	$51\frac{1}{2}$°N	Toronto	43°N
Tokyo	$35\frac{1}{2}$°N	Sydney	$33\frac{1}{2}$°S
New York	42°N	Peking	40°N
Auckland	37°S	Rome	42°N

B5 What is the latitude of the antipode of   (a) London   (b) Auckland

(See question A5 for the meaning of 'antipode'.)

61

C Longitude

The latitude of a place is a way of telling how far north or south it is from the equator.

Longitude is a way of telling how far east or west a place is. But east or west of where? We need a starting place for measuring east and west. This starting place is the **Greenwich meridian**.

Greenwich is a place in south-east London where a famous observatory used to be situated. The Greenwich meridian is the meridian which passes through the old observatory.

The position of the meridian at Greenwich itself is marked on a metal plate in the ground. If you go to Greenwich you can stand over the meridian, so that one half of you is east of the meridian and the other half is west.

This diagram shows the Greenwich meridian and another meridian.

The Greenwich meridian crosses the equator at A and the other meridian at B.
O is the centre of the Earth.

The angle AOB is the **longitude** of every point on the meridian through B.

Longitude can be measured **eastwards** or **westwards** from the Greenwich meridian.

This diagram shows some of the east and west meridians in the northern hemisphere.

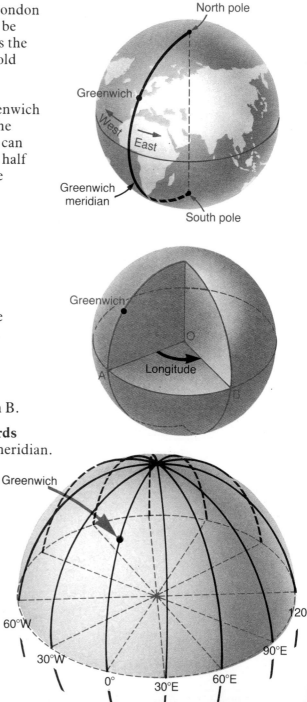

C1 Why is the 180°E meridian the same as the 180°W meridian?

C2 Each meridian forms half of a great circle.

Each meridian has an **anti-meridian** which forms the other half of the great circle.

Which meridian is the anti-meridian of

(a) the 30°W meridian (Look at the diagram at the bottom of the opposite page.)

(b) the 60°E meridian

(c) the Greenwich meridian

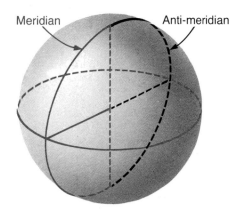

C3 The longitude of Athens is 24°E.
What is the longitude of the antipode of Athens?

The diagram below shows parallels of latitude and meridians in the northern hemisphere. The meridians cross the parallels of latitude at **right-angles**.

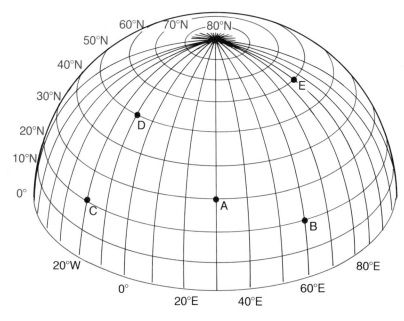

C4 Write down the latitude and longitude of the points marked A, B, C, D and E on the diagram.

C5 Write down the latitude and longitude of the antipode of each of the points A, B, C, D and E.

D Map projections

If the Earth were a cube, . . .   a cylinder, . . .   or a cone, . . .

its surface could be cut and flattened out to make a map.

But a sphere cannot be cut and flattened out, so it is not possible
to make a map of the world in this way.

A true representation of the shapes and sizes of continents, countries, seas,
and so on, can only be made on the surface of a sphere. A spherical 'map' of
the world is usually called a **globe**.

(If you have a globe to look at, you will find it useful in this section.)

The photo on the opposite page is a photo of a globe.
The photo is itself flat, so you can think of the photo as a 'map'
of the world.

The photo has been traced to make an ordinary outline map.
Look at this map carefully. The countries near the middle of this map
are much closer to their true shape than those near the edge.
This is because when you look at the globe the part closest to you (in the
middle of the map) is more nearly 'flat on' to you than the other parts
which curve away from you.

The map **distorts** the shapes of the countries. It distorts **all** the shapes, but
those near the middle are distorted less than those near the edge.

The map also distorts **areas**. It makes the countries near the edge look
much smaller than they really are in comparison with the countries
near the middle.

> **D1** On the map, the path shown in red looks like the shortest distance
> from A to B. Is this true on the surface of the globe? If not, why not?

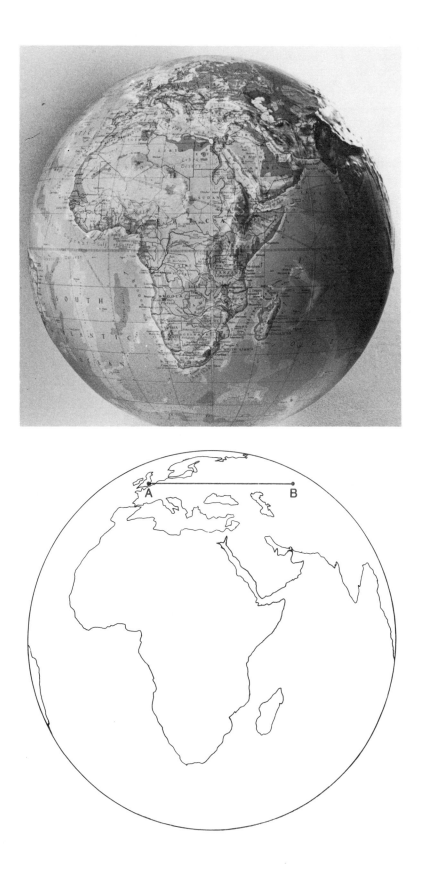

The first step in making a map of the world is to draw parallels of latitude and meridians.
We shall first of all describe a very simple way of doing this, and then point out the drawbacks.

1 Draw a straight line to represent the equator.

On the globe, the meridians at 0°, 30°, 60°, 90° etc. (east or west) are equally spaced along the equator. And they all cross the equator at right-angles.

Represent the meridians by straight lines at right-angles to the line representing the equator.

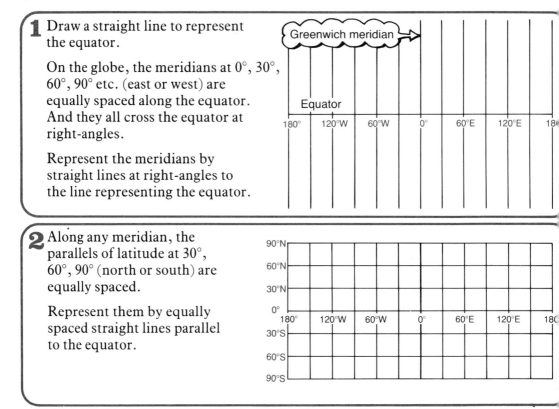

2 Along any meridian, the parallels of latitude at 30°, 60°, 90° (north or south) are equally spaced.

Represent them by equally spaced straight lines parallel to the equator.

When the outlines of continents are drawn on this grid, the map looks like this:

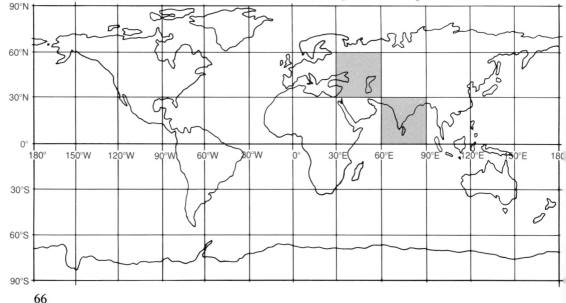

D2 The map opposite shows all meridians and parallels of latitude crossing at right-angles. Is this really true on the globe?

D3 On the map, the two shaded areas appear as equal. Are they equal on the globe? If not, which is larger?

D4 On the map, the 60°N parallel of latitude has the same length as the equator. Is this true on the globe?

D5 Where is the north pole on the map?

A method of representing the surface of the Earth on a flat, or plane, surface is called a **map projection**.

Because the surface of a sphere cannot be flattened out, all map projections involve distortion of some kind.

The projection used for the map opposite distorts **scale** (the parallels of latitude are not really all the same length), it distorts **area** and it distorts **shape**. But it does not distort the angles between meridians and parallels of latitude. We say the projection **preserves** this feature of the globe.

One way to modify the projection is to re-draw the parallels of latitude so that they are the correct length in relation to the equator.

There is a method for calculating the length of a parallel of latitude, using trigonometry.

Calculating the length of a parallel of latitude

In this diagram, P is a point on the 40°N parallel, or circle, of latitude.

The centre of the 40°N circle of latitude is C, which is a point on the Earth's axis.

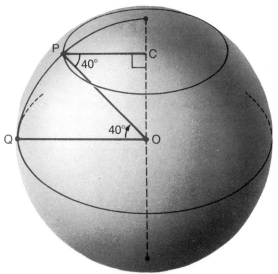

The meridian through P crosses the equator at Q. The centre of the Earth is O.

The angle QOP is 40° (the latitude of P).

So the angle OPC is also 40° (because QO is parallel to PC and the angles are alternate, or Z-angles).

Look at the **right-angled triangle OPC**. The hypotenuse, OP, is equal to the radius of the Earth, about 6400 km.

D6 The radius of the 40° circle of latitude is CP in the diagram. Explain how to calculate CP, and work out the circumference of the circle.

Here again is the diagram on the previous
page, but this time the latitude is called $\lambda°$
(the Greek letter l, called 'lambda').

The radius of the Earth is called R.

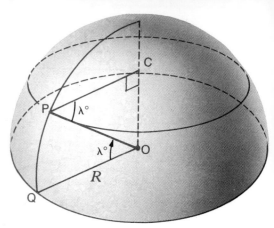

In the right-angled triangle OPC,
the hypotenuse, OP, is equal to R.

CP, the radius of the circle of latitude,
is the side adjacent to $\lambda°$.

Using the formula 'adj $=$ hyp $\times$ cosine', we get CP $= R \cos \lambda°$.

Writing this result in words, we get

the radius of the $\lambda°$ circle of latitude $= \cos \lambda° \times$ the radius of the Earth.

The length of the $\lambda°$ circle, or parallel, of latitude is the circumference of the circle.
To get the circumference we simply multiply the radius by 2π.

So it follows that

the length of the $\lambda°$ parallel of latitude $= \cos \lambda° \times$ the radius of the Earth $\times 2\pi$

$= \cos \lambda° \times$ the length of the equator.

D7 Calculate the length of each of these parallels of latitude.

(a) 30°   (b) 45°   (c) 60°   (d) 75°

We can now modify the map on page 66 so that the parallels of latitude are
the correct length in relation to the length of the equator.
As before, the meridians are equally spaced along each parallel of latitude.

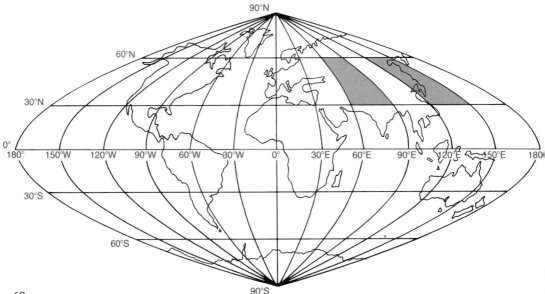

The projection shown at the bottom of the previous page is called the **Sanson–Flamsteed** projection.

It distorts shapes, especially near the edges of the map.
Distances along a parallel of latitude are correctly shown.
Distances along the central meridian are correctly shown but distances along other meridians are distorted.

The projection has an important feature: it preserves **area**.
Areas on the map are correctly shown in relation to one another. For example, the two shaded areas are equal on the map and also equal on the globe.
(This can be proved using more advanced mathematics.)

The central meridian does not have to be the 0° meridian. Any meridian can be taken as central meridian.

The distortion of shapes is not so great around the point where the central meridian crosses the equator. So the Sanson–Flamsteed projection is often used for maps of Africa, using a central meridian of 20°E.

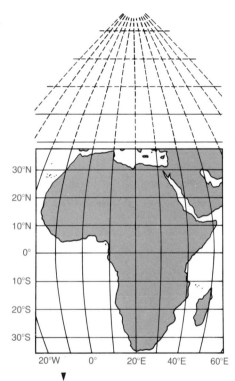

Some of the distortion in the map of the whole world can be lessened by splitting the map into several parts and using a different central meridian for each part.

When this is done we get a discontinuous or interrupted map like the one below.

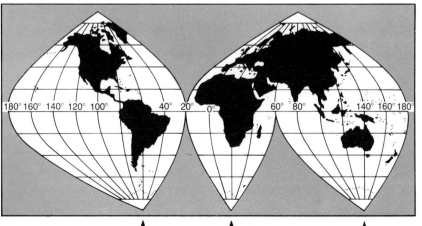

Central meridians marked ▲

Mercator's projection

Look back to the map at the bottom of page 66.
We saw that in this map the north and south parallels of latitude are shown longer than they really are, in relation to the equator.
The Sanson–Flamsteed projection is a way of putting this right.

There is another, rather different, way of tackling the problem and it leads to a method of projection called **Mercator's projection**.

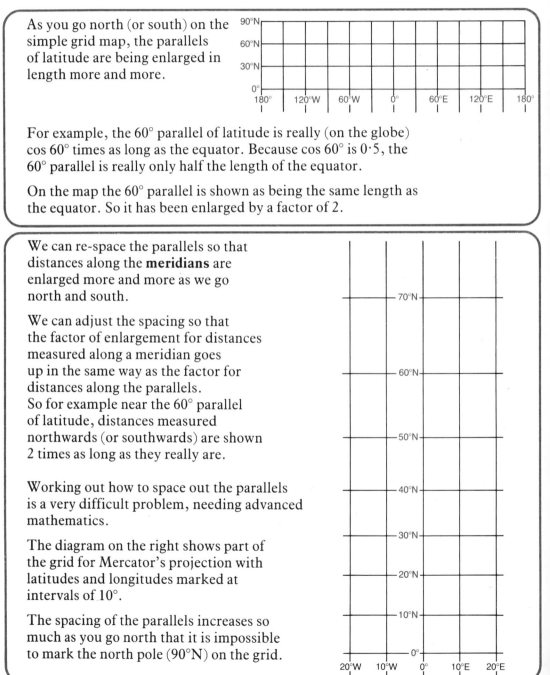

As you go north (or south) on the simple grid map, the parallels of latitude are being enlarged in length more and more.

For example, the 60° parallel of latitude is really (on the globe) cos 60° times as long as the equator. Because cos 60° is 0·5, the 60° parallel is really only half the length of the equator.

On the map the 60° parallel is shown as being the same length as the equator. So it has been enlarged by a factor of 2.

We can re-space the parallels so that distances along the **meridians** are enlarged more and more as we go north and south.

We can adjust the spacing so that the factor of enlargement for distances measured along a meridian goes up in the same way as the factor for distances along the parallels.
So for example near the 60° parallel of latitude, distances measured northwards (or southwards) are shown 2 times as long as they really are.

Working out how to space out the parallels is a very difficult problem, needing advanced mathematics.

The diagram on the right shows part of the grid for Mercator's projection with latitudes and longitudes marked at intervals of 10°.

The spacing of the parallels increases so much as you go north that it is impossible to mark the north pole (90°N) on the grid.

Here is a map which uses Mercator's projection.

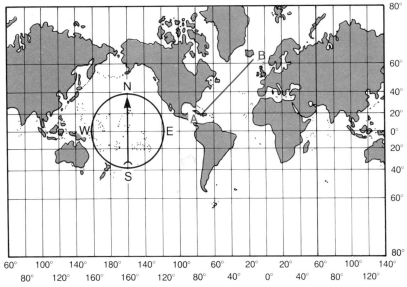

This map distorts distances because of the way the grid is constructed.
Take the British Isles, for example, which are quite close to the 60°N parallel
of latitude.
Near the 60°N parallel distances east–west and distances north–south are
both shown about twice as big as they should be (in relation to the equator).

So the British Isles are about twice as 'wide' and about twice as 'long' as
they should be, in comparison with a country near the equator.

This means that the area of the British Isles is shown on the map as
about four times what it should be.

Distortion of area increases the further you go from the equator. Greenland looks
about the same size as Africa. In fact its area is only about $\frac{1}{12}$ that of Africa!

Mercator's projection has an important feature which makes it useful:
it preserves **angles**. A Mercator map can be used to measure **bearings**.
(That is why a compass is marked on the map above.) For this reason
Mercator maps are useful in navigation.

For example, look at the path from A to B
marked on the map above. This path crosses
each meridian at 45°; the bearing of the
path is 045°.

If a ship starts at A on the Earth's surface
and always points in the direction 045°, it
will arrive at B. It will not travel by the
shortest route, even though on the map it
looks like the shortest route. But it is a
route which is easy to follow at sea, using a
magnetic compass.

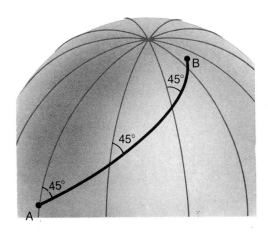

E Further map projections

In each of the projections we have looked at so far, we started with a straight line to represent the equator. The points where the meridians cross the equator were then spaced out equally along the line.

Another way is to start with a **pole**, say the north pole, and to draw the meridians as straight lines radiating out from it at equal angles. The circles of latitude can be represented by circles centred at the pole The only matter to be settled then is the spacing of the circles.

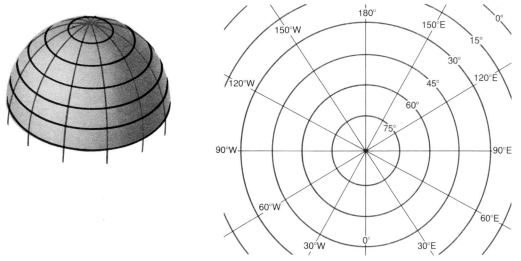

E1 On the globe, as you go along a meridian, the points where it crosses circles of latitude are equally spaced.
So one way to draw the map is to space the circles of latitude equally as shown above.

Does this method produce a true representation of the lengths of the circles of latitude? If not, why not?

If we draw the circles of latitude so that their lengths are correct in relation to one another, we get a map like the one on the right.

This projection is of no practical use.

E2 Why is the map on the right a **plan view** of the globe?

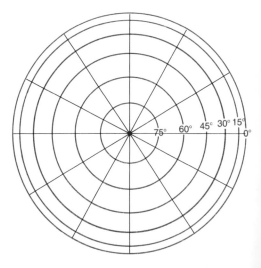

One particularly useful projection of the 'polar' type is called the **polar gnomonic projection**.

This time we shall let the south pole be the centre and explain how the projection is done.

This diagram shows a globe whose south pole touches a flat sheet of paper.

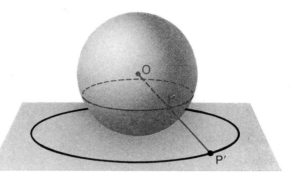

Let O be the centre of the globe and let P be a point on the surface of the globe.

The line OP is extended until it meets the paper at a point P'. P' is the point on the map which corresponds to P on the globe.

As P moves along a circle of latitude, so P' traces out a circle on the paper. This is the circle on the map which represents that circle of latitude.

This diagram shows how the spacing for the circles of latitude on the map can be found by drawing.

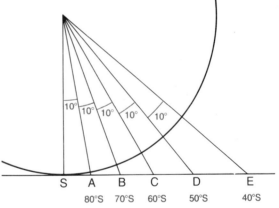

The circle in the diagram represents a cross-section of the Earth. It may be drawn any convenient size.

The distances SA, SB, SC, and so on, are the radii of the circles of latitude for 80°S, 70°S, 60°S, and so on.

The meridians are drawn as before, radiating out from the pole.

The polar gnomonic projection has a feature which makes it very useful in air navigation: great circle routes, which are the shortest routes on the globe, appear on the map as straight lines.

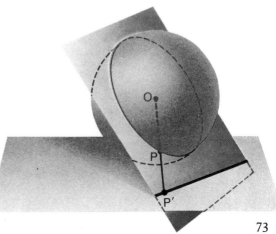

The reason for this is shown in the diagram here. A great circle is formed by a plane which goes through the centre of the Earth. This plane cuts the plane of the map in a straight line.

As the point P moves on the great circle, so P' moves along the line.

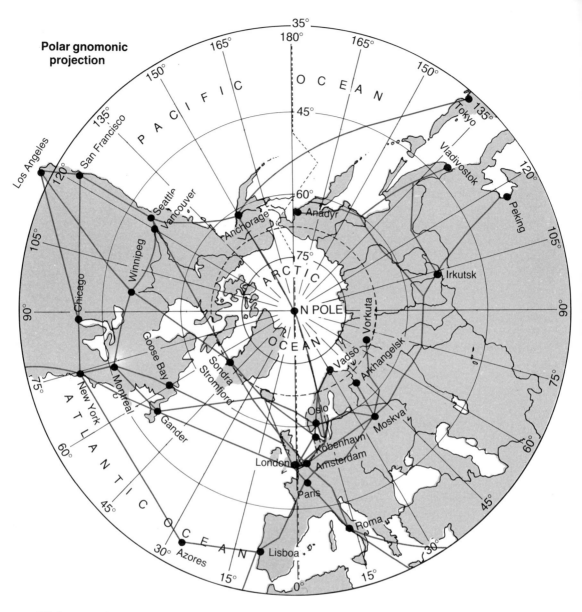

Polar gnomonic projection

This map shows some airline routes. The map uses the polar gnomonic projection, so great circle routes appear as straight lines. For example, the route from London to Gander is a great circle route.

Some other airline routes are not great circle routes and so are longer than they need be. This is sometimes for political reasons – planes may not be allowed to fly over certain countries. Sometimes it is for other reasons, such as avoiding areas of atmospheric disturbance.

E3 Lay a ruler along the great circle route from London to Tokyo. Estimate the most northerly latitude reached on this route.

E4 How can you tell that distances on this map are not shown correctly to scale?

When you travel abroad, you need to have foreign currency.

In France, you need French **francs**, in Italy you need **lire**, in Spain **pesetas**, etc.

You can 'buy' foreign currency from a bank or 'bureau de change'. The amount you get for every pound is called the exchange rate.

Exchange rates vary from day to day. Over long periods they may change quite considerably.

BUREAU DE CHANGE	
FRANCE	11·86
ITALY	2350
SPAIN	225
GREECE	151
GERMANY	3·89
HOLLAND	4·36
AUSTRIA	27·25
USA	1·45
CANADA	1·80

1   If the exchange rates are as shown in the picture above, how many French francs would you get for   (a) £50   (b) £80

2   How much would you have to pay (in £) for 500 francs?

3   In France, a restaurant advertises three set menus, costing 35F, 54F and 72F. Calculate the cost of each of these in pounds and pence.

Travellers' cheques are a good way to take money abroad. You can change them for money when you get there. Each cheque is for your own personal use only, and if you lose one you do not lose any money, provided you report the loss quickly.

Travellers' cheques can be issued in £ sterling, US dollars, French francs, etc.

When you change money, the bank or bureau de change charges you a small amount (called 'commission') for the transaction.

When you leave the foreign country, or when you get home, you may have some foreign money left. If you go to change it back into Sterling, you will find that the exchange rates for changing foreign money into Sterling are slightly different from the rates for changing Sterling into foreign money. From your point of view the rates are slightly worse: you don't get back quite as much as you would expect.

7 Equations and graphs

A The graph of $y = ax$

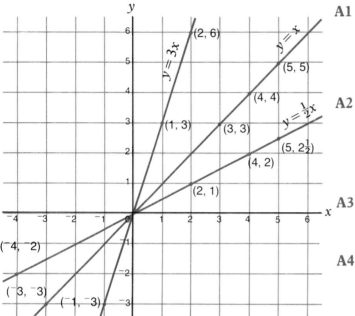

A1 The diagram shows the graphs of $y = 3x$, $y = x$ and $y = \frac{1}{2}x$.

Write down the gradient of each graph.

A2 (a) Draw the graphs of

      (i) $y = 2x$ (ii) $y = {}^-3x$

(b) Write down the gradient of each graph.

A3 Describe in words the graph of

(a) $y = 100x$ (b) $y = {}^-100x$

A4 Explain why the graph of $y = ax$ goes through $(0, 0)$, whatever the value of a.

The graph of $y = ax$ is a straight line through $(0, 0)$ with gradient a.

If a is positive, the line slopes upwards from left to right.

If a is negative, the line slopes downwards from left to right.

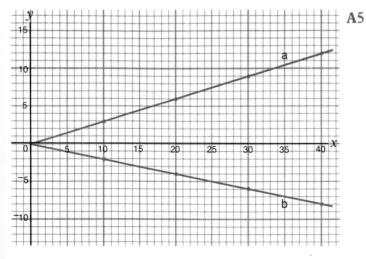

A5 (a) Find the gradient of each of these graphs.

(b) Write the equation of each graph.

B The graph of $y = ax + b$

Here is the graph of $y = \frac{1}{2}x$.

If we change the equation to $y = \frac{1}{2}x + 2$, every point on $y = \frac{1}{2}x$ moves up 2 units.

The **intercept** on the y-axis is now 2. The gradient is still $\frac{1}{2}$.

If we change the equation to $y = \frac{1}{2}x - 2$, every point on $y = \frac{1}{2}x$ moves down 2 units.

The intercept on the y-axis is now $^-2$. The gradient is still $\frac{1}{2}$.

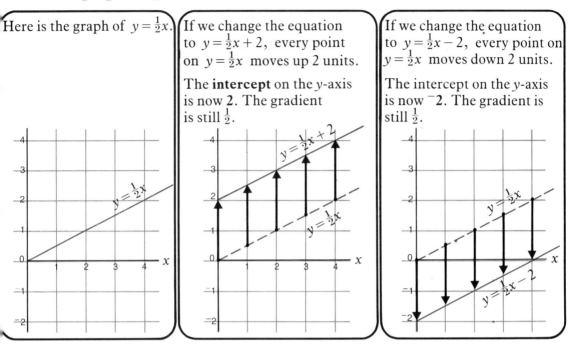

B1 All of the lines in the diagram on the right have a gradient of $\frac{1}{3}$.

For each line, write down

(i) its intercept on the y-axis

(ii) its equation

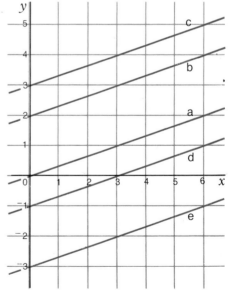

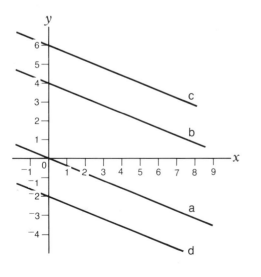

B2 All the lines in the diagram on the left have gradient $^-0.4$.

Write down the equation of each line.

77

> The graph of $y = ax + b$ is a straight line of gradient a, whose intercept on the y-axis is b.

Worked example

Find the equation of the line shown here.

First we need to find the gradient of the line. To do this, choose two points on the line (the further apart the better, for accuracy). Here we have chosen the points marked A, B.

From A to B is 30 across and 9 down. So the gradient of AB is $\dfrac{-9}{30} = {}^-0\cdot3$.

The intercept of the line on the y-axis is **11**.

So the equation of the line is $y = {}^-0\cdot3x + 11$.

B3 Calculate the gradient of each of these lines, and write down the equation of each line.

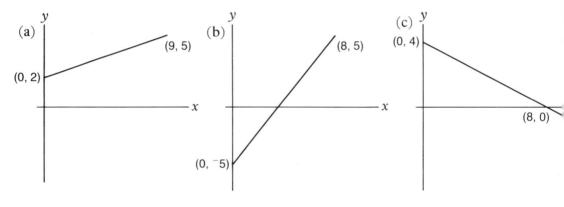

B4 Find the equation of each of these lines.

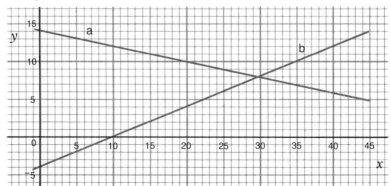

C The graphs of $y = ax^2$ and $y = \dfrac{a}{x}$

C1 Draw axes on graph paper, with x from $^-2$ to 2 and y from $^-2$ to 6, using 2 cm for 1 unit on both axes.

Here is a table of values for the equation $y = x^2$.

x	$^-2$	$^-1\cdot5$	$^-1$	$^-0\cdot5$	0	$0\cdot5$	1	$1\cdot5$	2
y	4	$2\cdot25$	1	$0\cdot25$	0	$0\cdot25$	1	$2\cdot25$	4

(a) Draw the graph of $y = x^2$ and label it.

(b) Multiply the values in the second line of the table by $1\cdot5$. Draw the graph of $y = 1\cdot5x^2$ and label it.

(c) Multiply the values in the second line of the table by $^-0\cdot5$. Draw and label the graph of $y = {}^-0\cdot5x^2$.

The graphs you drew in question C1 show the general shape of the graph of $y = ax^2$.

The graph of $y = ax^2$ is a curve which touches the x-axis at $(0, 0)$ and gets steeper and steeper further away from $(0, 0)$.

The graph of $y = ax^2$

a positive a negative

C2 This is a sketch of the graph of $y = \tfrac{1}{2}x^2$.

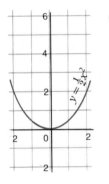

Copy the sketch and add to it the graphs of $y = \tfrac{1}{2}x^2 + 3$ and $y = \tfrac{1}{2}x^2 - 2$, showing clearly how they are related to the graph of $y = \tfrac{1}{2}x^2$.

C3 Draw axes on graph paper with x and y from $^-6$ to 6, using 1 cm to 1 unit on both axes.

(a) You are going to draw the graph of $y = \dfrac{3}{x}$. Calculate the value of y when x is 6, 5, 4, 3, 2, $1\cdot5$, 1 and $0\cdot5$, and make a table of values.

(b) Why is there no value of y when x is 0?

(c) Continue the table of values to show the value of y when x is $^-0\cdot5$, $^-1$, $^-1\cdot5$, $^-2$, $^-3$, $^-4$, $^-5$ and $^-6$.

(d) Draw the graph of $y = \dfrac{3}{x}$.

This diagram shows the graphs of $y = \dfrac{3}{x}$ and of $y = \dfrac{12}{x}$.

Each graph is in two parts.

As x increases, the graphs get closer and closer to the x-axis, but never reach it.

Other graphs of the form $y = \dfrac{a}{x}$ have the same kind of shape. If a is negative, the graph occupies the other two 'quadrants', like this.

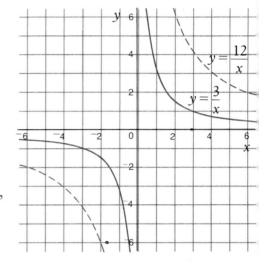

C4 A girl was asked to draw sketch graphs of these equations:

$$y = 2 \cdot 5x \qquad y = 0 \cdot 8x \qquad y = 1 \cdot 5x - 2 \qquad y = 4 - 0 \cdot 6x$$

$$y = 0 \cdot 8x^2 \qquad y = 0 \cdot 3x^2 + 4 \qquad y = 4 - 0 \cdot 3x^2 \qquad y = \dfrac{2}{x}$$

She drew them all correctly, but forgot to label them. Which of the equations goes with each graph?

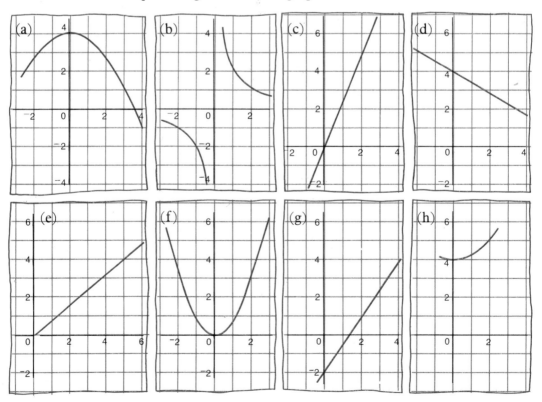

D Fitting a linear equation

In a chemistry experiment, potassium bromide was dissolved in 100 g of water at 0 °C. The mass which could be dissolved was measured. Then the experiment was repeated at various different temperatures.

These were the results obtained. t stands for the temperature in °C and m for the mass in grams which could be dissolved.

t	0	19	41	60	80
m	53·4	64·1	75·2	84·7	95·5

If we look at the table, there does not seem to be any obvious relationship between t and m. But if we plot the values of (t, m) on a graph, then a relationship is suggested.

The points do not lie exactly on a straight line, but the dotted line drawn here fits them quite well.

The dotted line is a 'line of best fit'.

The equation of the line will be of the form

$$m = at + b$$

where a is the gradient and b is the intercept on the m-axis.
(The equation is derived from $y = ax + b$ by writing t instead of x, and m instead of y.)

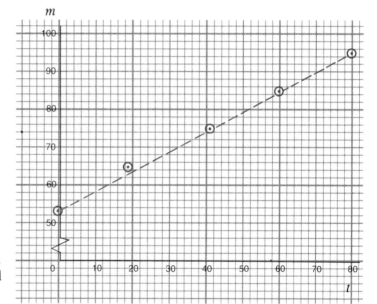

D1 (a) Find the gradient of the dotted line of best fit.

(b) Write down its intercept on the y-axis.

(c) Write down the equation of the line.

D2 A similar experiment, but this time using sodium nitrate, gave these results.

t	0	20	32	40
m	72·9	87·5	96·3	102

(a) Plot the four pairs of values of (t, m) on a graph, and draw a line of best fit.

(b) Find the equation of your line of best fit.

81

D3 This table shows pairs of measurements of two variables p and q.

p	12·0	15·3	17·8	19·0
q	24·4	29·0	32·6	34·2

(a) Plot the four points on a (p, q) graph and draw a line of best fit.

(b) Find the equation of your line of best fit.

D4 Repeat question D3 for this table.

p	50·0	62·4	80·5	97·0
q	7·50	6·50	5·05	3·75

E Fitting other equations

Suppose we use the method described in the previous section to the data in this table.

p	1·3	1·9	2·5	3·1	3·8	4·4
q	14·6	18·5	23·7	30·5	40·1	50·0

We start by drawing the graph of (p, q).

This time the graph is not a straight line.
It curves upwards, getting steeper and steeper,
and this suggests an equation with p^2 in it.

It can't be of the form $q = ap^2$, because
that would go through $(0, 0)$, . . .

but it might be of the form $q = ap^2 + b$.

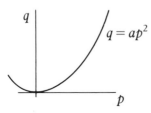

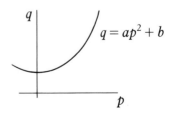

There is a method of 'transforming' a graph of the form $q = ap^2 + b$ into a straight-line graph.

We first compare the equation $q = ap^2 + b$ with the standard straight-line equation $y = ax + b$:

$$q = a\,p^2 + b$$
$$\downarrow \qquad \downarrow$$
$$y = a\,x + b$$

We let x be p^2, and y be q. We make a new table of values.

$x (= p^2)$	1·69	3·61	6·25	9·61	14·44	19·36
$y (= q)$	14·6	18·5	23·7	30·5	40·1	50·0

These are the squares of the values of p in the original table.

Now we draw the graph of (x, y), with a line of best fit.

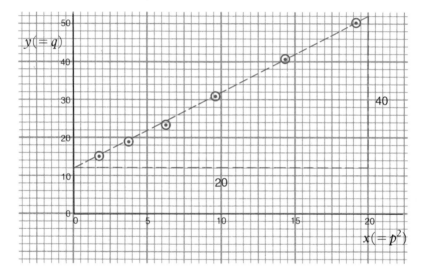

As before, we find the gradient and intercept of this line.
Its gradient is $\frac{40}{20} = 2$. The intercept on the y-axis is **12**.

So the equation of the line is $y = 2x + 12$.

Now remember that x stands for p^2 and y stands for q; so the equation connecting q and p is

$$q = 2p^2 + 12.$$

E1 This table shows pairs of values of two variables p and q.

p	3·0	4·6	5·2	6·0	7·4
q	24·5	30·6	33·5	38·0	47·4

It is thought that there is a relationship between p and q, of the form $q = ap^2 + b$. Let x be p^2 and y be q; make a table of values of (x, y), draw a graph and use it to find a and b.

83

E2 Two variables S and T are believed to be related by an equation of the form $T = aS^2 + b$.

Here are some pairs of values of S and T.

S	1·5	2·5	3·0	4·0	4·5
T	31·6	25·6	21·5	11·0	4·6

By drawing a suitable graph, find the values of a and b.

The method can be extended to other kinds of relationship.

Suppose p and q are connected by an equation of the form $q = ap^3 + b$. We compare this equation with the standard straight-line equation.

$$q = a p^3 + b$$
$$\downarrow \quad \downarrow$$
$$y = a x + b$$

This tells us to let x be p^3, and y be q. We will then get a straight-line graph from which we can find the values of a and b.

If the equation connecting p and q is of the form $q = a\sqrt{p} + b$, we would let x be $\sqrt{p}$ and y be q.

If the equation is of the form $q = \dfrac{a}{p} + b$, or $q = a\left(\dfrac{1}{p}\right) + b$, we would let x be $\dfrac{1}{p}$ and y be q.

E3 Two variables p and q are connected by an equation of the form $q = a\sqrt{p} + b$. Here are some pairs of values of p and q.

p	1·4	3·3	7·2	10·6	15·8
q	11·5	13·0	15·2	16·6	18·4

(a) Let $x = \sqrt{p}$ and $y = q$. Make a table of values of x and y.

(b) Draw the graph of (x, y) and use it to find the values of a and b.

(c) Check that the equation $q = a\sqrt{p} + b$ fits the numbers in the original table.

E4 Two variables R and S are connected by an equation of the form $S = \dfrac{a}{R} + b$.

Here are some values of R and S.

R	1·2	1·5	2·0	2·5	3·0
S	6·4	4·4	2·4	1·2	0·4

By drawing a suitable graph, find the values of a and b.

8 Three dimensions

A Perspective

Look directly at a door (or window) of the room where you are working.

Shut one eye and hold a pencil in front of you, so that the pencil's length appears to coincide with the height of the door.

You are not fooled into thinking that the pencil and the door are of equal height. You know that the heights look the same because the pencil is much closer to your eye than the door.

But why does a large object at a distance appear to be the same size as a small object close to you? The diagram below explains why. It is a side view of someone doing what you have just done.

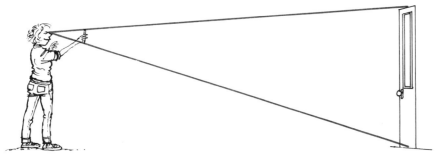

The top of the pencil and the top of the door are in line with the person's eye. So are the bottom of the pencil and the bottom of the door.

Any other object placed exactly between these lines will appear to have the same height as both the door and the pencil.

A1 An insect on the ground sees this view of a garden gnome and a birdbath.
The birdbath is 100 cm tall and the gnome is 40 cm tall. They are 200 cm apart.
Draw a 'side view' to show where the insect is in relation to the gnome and the birdbath.

A girl looks out of a plate glass window and sees a bus outside. What she sees is shown in the picture on the right.

The bus appears to be about half the height of the window.

A side view of the girl, the window and the bus is shown below.
The points P and Q show where the top and bottom of the bus appear on the window.

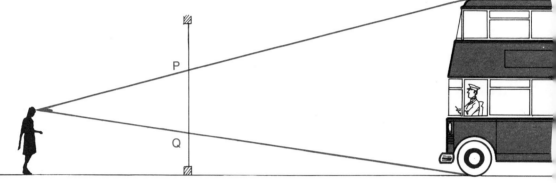

As the bus moves closer, P moves up and Q moves down. The bus appears to get larger.

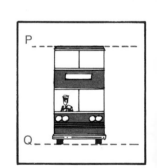

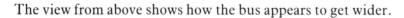

The view from above shows how the bus appears to get wider.

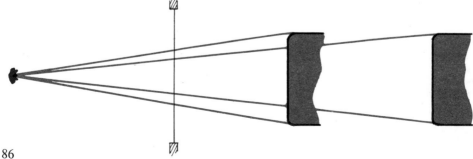

A2 Karen is looking through a window at a flagpole outside.
The flagpole is 3 m tall and 4 m from the window
The window is 2 m tall.
Karen is standing 1·5 m from the window. Her eyes are
1 m above the ground.

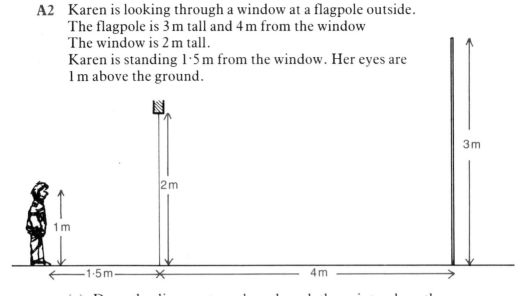

(a) Draw the diagram to scale and mark the points where the
top and bottom of the flagpole appear on the window.

(b) Draw a sketch, as accurately as you can, of the window and
flagpole as Karen sees them. (The window is 200 cm wide.)

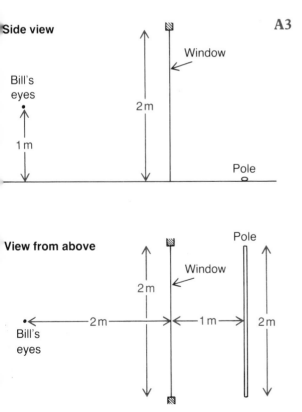

A3 Bill is looking out through a window
at a pole which is lying on the ground
outside, parallel to the window.

The drawings on the left show two
views of the situation, a side view
and a view from above.

(a) Draw the view from above to scale.
Mark the points where the two ends
of the pole appear on the window.

(b) Draw the side view to scale.
Mark the point where the pole
appears on the window.

(c) From your two drawings you have
enough information to make a
drawing of the window and pole
as Bill sees them. Do this.

When we look at things in the ordinary way, the view of them which we see is called a **perspective** view. A photo taken by an ordinary camera is also a perspective view.

We have been seeing perspective views all our lives, so we have got used to them. We know that an object appears to get smaller as it moves away from us. The reason why this happens has already been explained.

Another well-known feature of perspective views is illustrated in this picture.

We know that the rails are really parallel to each other, although they appear to converge towards a point.

But why do they appear to do this? We can explain why by using the idea of looking through a glass window.

In the diagram below, the rails are horizontal and the direction in which the person is looking is horizontal as well.

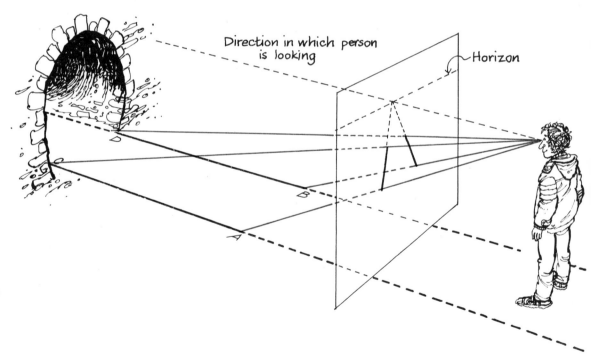

The points A and B on the ground are really the same distance apart as C and D. But A and B are closer to the person than C and D. In the picture, AB looks larger than CD, and the rails appear to converge.

The point where the rails appear to meet is at the level of the person's eyes. The horizontal line at this level in the picture is called the **horizon**.

Think of a person looking through a window as in the previous diagrams. Suppose the direction in which he or she is looking is **horizontal** and at right-angles to the plane of the window.

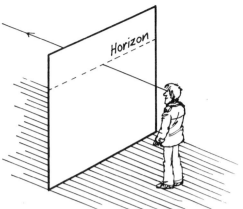

The window forms what is called a **picture plane**. It is a plane at right-angles to the direction in which the person is looking.

Here are some of the 'rules of perspective' which apply to the views the person sees when the picture plane is vertical.

1 Vertical lines appear vertical.
Equally spaced points on a vertical line appear equally spaced.

2 Horizontal lines which are parallel to the picture plane appear horizontal.
Equally spaced points on these lines appear equally spaced.

Horizon

3 Other horizontal lines which are parallel to each other meet on the horizon.
The point where they meet is called a **vanishing point**.

Horizon   Vanishing point

4 Equally spaced points on one of these lines do not appear equally spaced.

They appear to get closer together the further away they are.

Perspective problems *(The diagrams for these problems are on worksheet Y5-1.)*

A4 Show how to finish this perspective drawing of a cuboid.

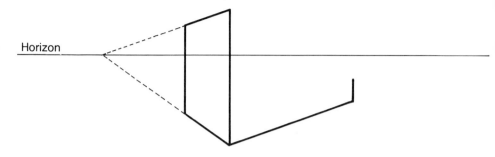

A5 This is a perspective view of a horizontal rectangle ABCD.

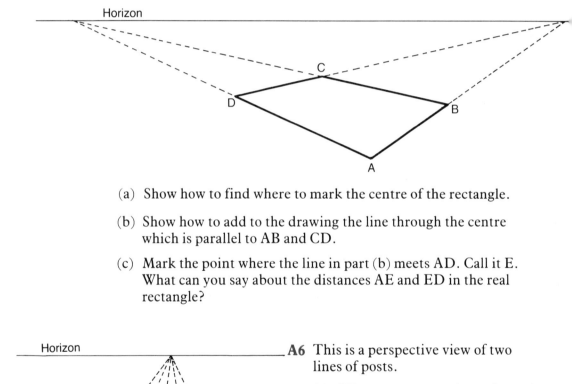

(a) Show how to find where to mark the centre of the rectangle.

(b) Show how to add to the drawing the line through the centre which is parallel to AB and CD.

(c) Mark the point where the line in part (b) meets AD. Call it E. What can you say about the distances AE and ED in the real rectangle?

A6 This is a perspective view of two lines of posts.

(a) What can you say about the real lines AA′, BB′, CC′, DD′ and EE′?

(b) The posts at A, B, C, D and E are equally spaced. Are the posts at A′, B′, C′, D′ and E′ equally spaced?

(c) Draw a sketch of what the two lines of posts look like from above. Show the dotted lines in your sketch.

A7 The two lamp-posts in this perspective view are of equal height.

(a) Show how to draw the horizon.

(b) Show how to draw another lamp-post whose base is at the point A and which is the same height as the other two.

A8 This is a perspective view of two trees. Which is taller?
Show how you can tell which is taller.

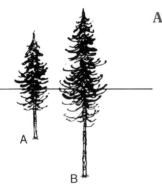

A9 The two lamp-posts in this perspective drawing are of equal height.

(a) Show how to draw the horizon.

(b) Show how to draw a third lamp-post at A which is the same height as the other two.

A10 The height of the front two towers of this cathedral is 30 metres.

Show how you can use the perspective drawing to find the height of the spire.

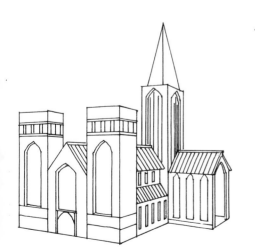

So far we have considered perspective views for a person looking in a horizontal direction. The same rules apply when a camera points in a horizontal direction.

If a camera points in a horizontal direction, the picture plane is vertical, so vertical lines appear vertical.

If the camera is tilted upwards, the picture plane is no longer vertical, and vertical lines appear to converge upwards.

If the camera is tilted downwards, vertical lines appear to converge downwards.

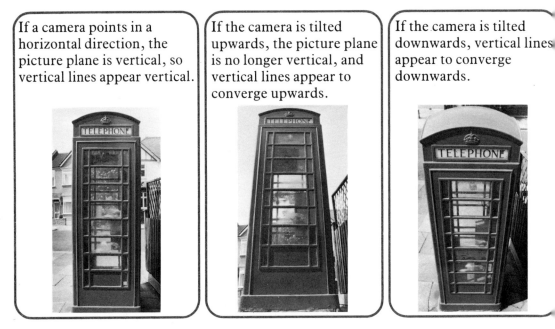

Here for example is a perspective view of a horizontal matchbox, as seen by someone looking down at an angle to the horizontal.

The picture plane here is not vertical, so vertical lines appear to converge at a vanishing point.

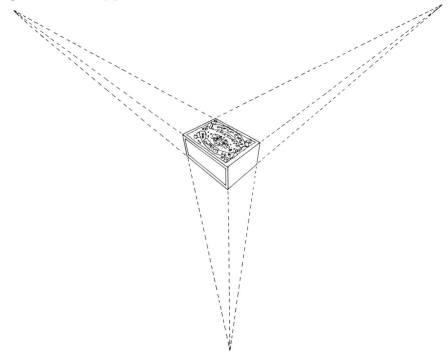

B Orthographic projection

This diagram shows how a perspective
view of a table is formed.

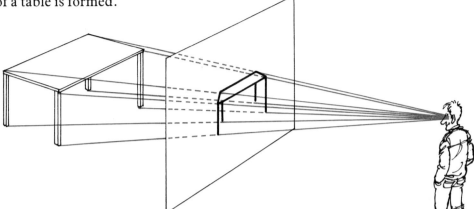

The red lines from the table through the picture plane meet at
the person's eye.

Suppose we draw these lines so that they are all at
right-angles to the picture plane, like this.

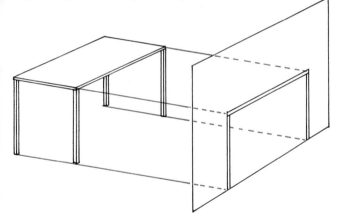

This kind of 'view' of the table
is called an **orthographic
projection**.

Notice a big difference between the perspective view and the orthographic
projection.

 In the perspective view
you can see all four
legs of the table.

In the orthographic
projection, the back
legs are exactly
hidden by the front
legs.

The orthographic projection is not a view you could ever actually **see**.
But if you are a long way away from the table, the front legs can **almost**
hide the back legs.

Orthographic projections are used a great deal by architects, designers and engineers. This is because it is possible to take accurate measurements from orthographic projections.

Usually, three orthographic projections of an object are enough to give a 'total picture' of it.

They are called a **plan** (from above), and **elevations** (usually from the front and side).

Orthographic projections are often called 'views'.

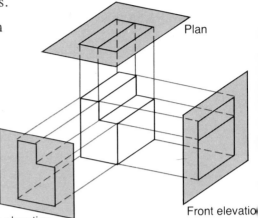

Plan

Side elevation

Front elevation

B1 Here are a plan and two elevations of a shed, drawn to a scale of 1 cm to 1 m.

The roof (shaded) is covered with roofing felt.

A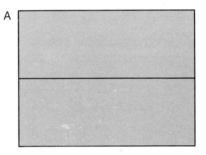

B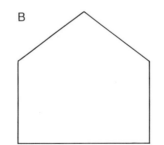

C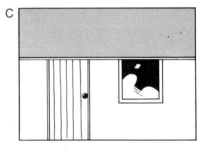

(a) Which of the three views, A, B, C could be used to measure the height of the shed?

(b) Calculate the area of the roofing felt. Explain carefully how you do it.

B2 Draw roughly a plan and two elevations of each of these objects.

(a) (b)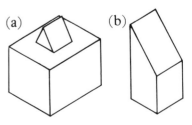

B3 Here are three full-size orthographic projections of a 3-pin plug.

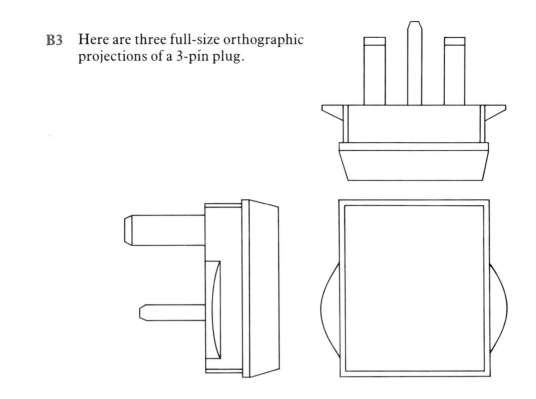

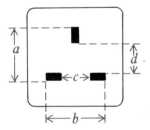

(a) The diagram on the left shows a socket which the plug will fit. What are the full-size measurements a, b, c, d?

(b) The diagram below shows a double socket into which two of the plugs will fit. What is the smallest that e can be?

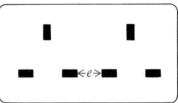

Dotted lines are often used to show features which are out of sight. For example, here are two views of a hollow cylinder.

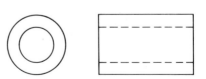

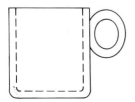

B4 This is a side view of an object. Sketch a plan view.

'Shadows'

If an object is placed in a parallel beam of light, and a shadow is cast on a plane at right-angles to the beam, the shadow is an orthographic projection of the object (but without any detail).

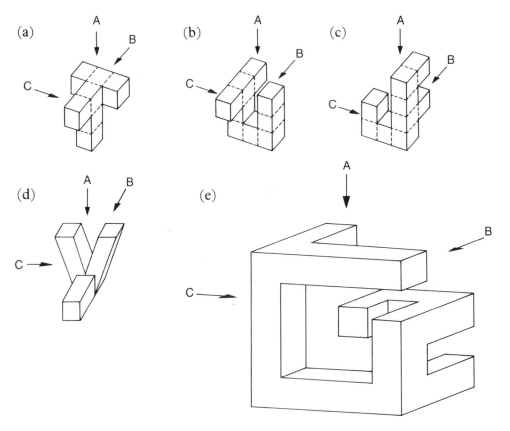

B5 Sketch the shadow you would get if the object in the diagram above were illuminated by a parallel beam from above.

B6 Sketch the shadows obtained by illuminating each of these objects in each of the directions A (from above), B and C (horizontally).

(a)

(b)

(c)

(d)

(e)

B7 Sketch a single object which can give these three shadows.

C Other kinds of projection

Perspective views show objects as they really appear, but they are difficult to draw accurately.
Orthogonal projections are easier to draw, but you need several different views of an object to get a 'total picture'.

There are other ways of representing three-dimensional objects in two-dimensional drawings. Here we show a matchbox drawn in three different ways.

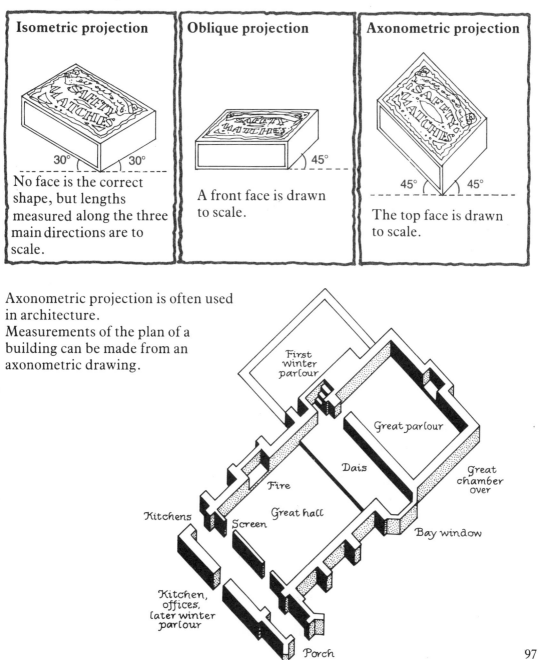

Isometric projection	Oblique projection	Axonometric projection
30° 30°	45°	45° 45°
No face is the correct shape, but lengths measured along the three main directions are to scale.	A front face is drawn to scale.	The top face is drawn to scale.

Axonometric projection is often used in architecture.
Measurements of the plan of a building can be made from an axonometric drawing.

First winter parlour

Great parlour

Dais

Great chamber over

Fire

Great hall

Bay window

Kitchens

Screen

Kitchen, offices, later winter parlour

Porch

97

D Coordinates in three dimensions

So far in this chapter we have looked at ways of representing objects
in three-dimensional space by two-dimensional drawings.

Another way to represent three-dimensional space is by numbers.

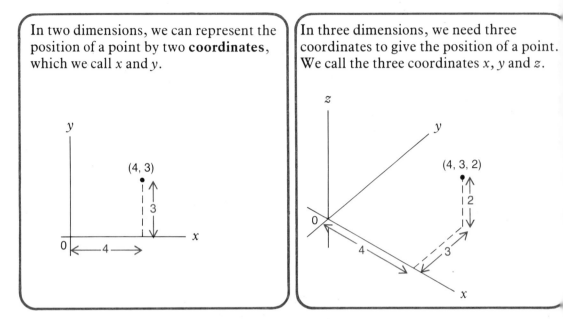

In two dimensions, we can represent the
position of a point by two **coordinates**,
which we call x and y.

In three dimensions, we need three
coordinates to give the position of a point.
We call the three coordinates x, y and z.

It often helps to think of the plane containing the x- and y-axes
as a horizontal plane. The z-coordinate then tells us how far a point
is above (or below) the 'xy'-plane. So if a point is actually in the xy-plane,
its z-coordinate is 0.

For example, at the point C in this diagram,
the x-coordinate is 3 and the y-coordinate is 3.
The z-coordinate at C is 0, so C is $(3, 3, 0)$.

G is 3 units above C, so G is $(3, 3, 3)$.

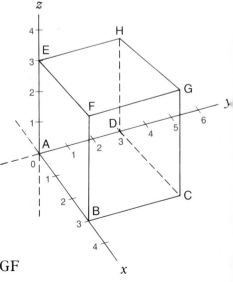

D1 Write down the coordinates of
A, B, C, D, E, F, G, and H.

D2 Write down the coordinates
of the midpoint of

(a) EH (b) FG (c) AC

D3 Write down the coordinates
of the centre of the face

(a) ABFE (b) DCGH (c) BCGF

D4 Write down the coordinates of the centre of the cube.

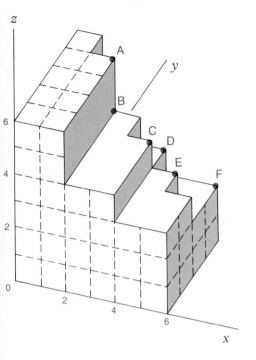

D5 Write down the coordinates of the points marked A to F in the diagram on the left.

D6 Calculate the lengths PQ, QR and PR in the diagram below.

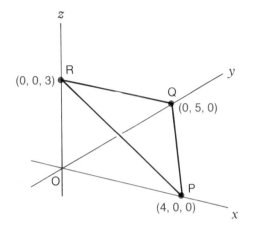

D7 The diagram on the left shows a house with an extension.

(a) Write down the coordinates of the points marked A, B and C.

(b) D is the midpoint of a sloping edge of the roof of the house. Work out the coordinates of D.

(c) The measurements are all in metres. Calculate the length of the sloping edge *a* of the extension roof.

(d) Calculate the angle the edge *a* makes with the horizontal.

(e) Calculate the length of each of the four sloping edges of the roof of the house.

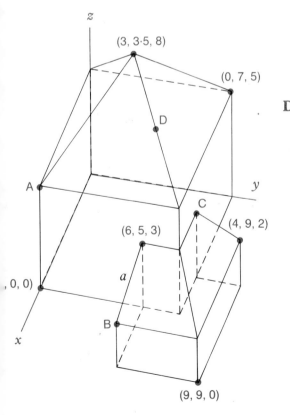

99

THREE-DIMENSIONAL PUZZLES

1   The letters of the word 'PUZZLES' above are drawings of 'three-dimensional letters'.

The drawings below are plan views of three-dimensional letters. No hidden edges are shown. What letter(s) could each plan represent?

Sketch each letter you can think of. There may be more than one way of making some letters. For example, an 'A' could have a flat top   or a pointed top.

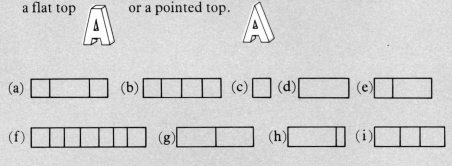

(a)   (b)   (c)   (d)   (e)

(f)   (g)   (h)   (i)

2   The drawings below are a plan and an elevation of a solid object (**not** a cube or other object with squares drawn on it!) 'Hidden edges' are not shown because there aren't any.

Draw a sketch of the object to show its shape.

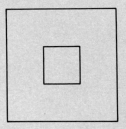

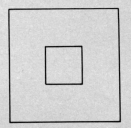

5 The sine and cosine functions (1)

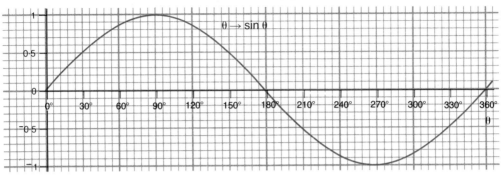

5.1 This is the graph of the function $\theta \rightarrow \sin \theta$ for values of θ from $0°$ to $360°$.

(a) From the graph find approximately the values of θ for which $\sin \theta = 0·6$.

(b) If you use a calculator to find inv sin $0·6$ you get only one angle, $36·9°$ (to 1 d.p.). What is the other angle, also correct to 1 d.p.?

5.2 Copy this sketch of the graph of $\theta \rightarrow \sin \theta$, and sketch on the same axes the graph of $\theta \rightarrow \cos \theta$. Label both graphs.

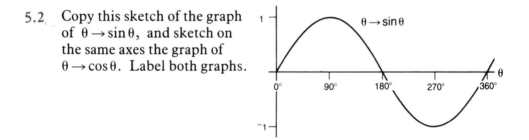

5.3 Find two angles in the range $0°$ to $360°$ whose cosines are $0·75$. Give each answer to the nearest degree.

5.4 Find, to the nearest degree, two angles in the range $0°$ to $360°$ whose sines are $0·25$.

5.5 Find two values of θ in the range $0°$ to $360°$ which satisfy each of these equations.

(a) $\sin \theta = 0·44$ (b) $\cos \theta = 0·69$

(c) $\sin \theta = {}^-0·34$ (d) $\cos \theta = {}^-0·83$

(e) $\cos \theta = 0·09$ (f) $\cos \theta = {}^-0·09$

(g) $\sin \theta = 0·09$ (h) $\sin \theta = {}^-0·09$

6 The Earth

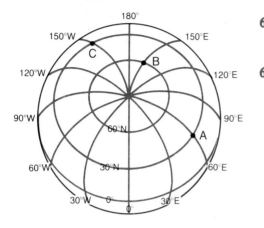

6.1 Write down the latitude and longitude of each of the points marked A, B and C.

6.2 The antipode of a point is the point which is diametrically opposite it on the Earth's surface. (If you draw a line from the point through the centre of the Earth, the line meets the surface again at the antipode of the point.)

Write down the latitude and longitude of the antipodes of A, B and C.

6.3 Taking the radius of the Earth as 3960 miles, calculate the great circle distance from the point A in the diagram to

(a) the north pole　　(b) the south pole　　(c) the antipode of A

7 Equations and graphs

7.1 (a) What is the gradient of line a in this diagram?

(b) Write down the equation of line a.

(c) Write down the equation of line b.

(d) Write down the equation of line c.

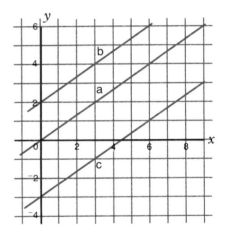

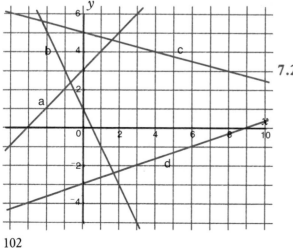

7.2 Write down

(i) the gradient

(ii) the intercept on the y-axis

(iii) the equation

of each line shown in this diagram.

7.3 Diagrams A to L below are rough sketches of the graphs of the following equations:

$$y = 2 + \tfrac{1}{2}x \qquad y = 2 - \tfrac{1}{2}x \qquad y = \tfrac{1}{2}x - 2 \qquad y = \tfrac{1}{2}x^2$$

$$y = 2x^2 \qquad y = 2 + x^2 \qquad y = 2 - x^2 \qquad y = x^2 - 2$$

$$y = \frac{2}{x} \qquad y = \frac{^-2}{x} \qquad y = 2 - 2x \qquad y = 2 + 2x$$

Match the correct equation to each sketch.

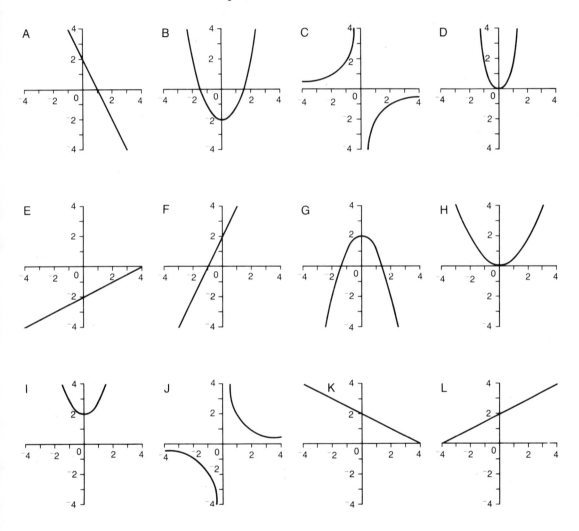

7.4 The following data is believed to fit approximately an equation of the form $Q = aP + b$.

P	4·0	5·8	6·9	8·8	10·0
Q	15·6	14·7	14·0	13·0	12·2

Draw a line of best fit and use it to find values for a and b.

7.5 The following data is believed to fit approximately an equation of the form $v = au^2 + b$.

u	0·7	1·2	2·2	2·6	3·0	3·5
v	⁻4·3	⁻2·8	2·3	5·1	8·5	13·4

Draw a suitable straight-line graph and use it to find values for a and b.

8 Three dimensions

8.1 These drawings show a front elevation and a side elevation of a workshop. They are drawn to a scale of 1 cm to 1 m.

 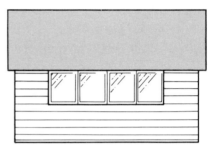

(a) Find the area of the floor of the workshop.

(b) The roof is covered with roofing felt. Find the area of the roofing felt.

8.2 Draw full-size a plan view, a front elevation and a left-side elevation of the solid shown here.

(All measurements are in mm.)

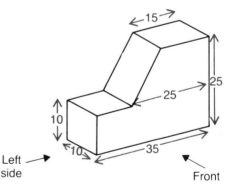

8.3 One edge of a cuboid is from $(0, 0, 0)$ to $(2, 0, 0)$. Another is from $(0, 0, 0)$ to $(0, 4, 0)$. Another is from $(0, 0, 0)$ to $(0, 0, 5)$. Write down the coordinates of the other four corners of the cuboid.

9 Iteration

A The limit of a sequence

A1 Generate a familiar sequence of numbers by following the instructions in this flowchart.

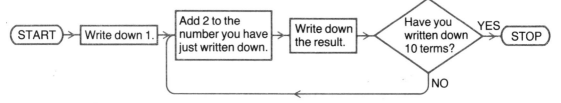

What you have just done is a simple example of an **iterative** process.
Each time you go round the loop, you follow the same set of instructions.

The diagram on the right shows what an iterative process is.
Each output becomes the input for the next calculation.

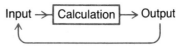

Iterative processes have become very important in the last thirty years, since the introduction of computers.
Weather forecasts, for example, are now prepared using iterative methods on a high-speed computer. Weather information from all over the northern hemisphere is fed into the computer and the weather patterns are calculated for one minute later. The new weather patterns are then fed in to find the weather patterns another minute later. This goes on until a 24-hour forecast has been produced.

The work could be done by people, but by the time they finished, the forecast would be at least several months out of date!

You can think of the computer as producing a sequence of forecasts in the same way that you have just produced a sequence of numbers.

The sequence in question A1 is generated by adding 2 to each term to get the next term.
If we let u_n stand for the nth term of the sequence, and u_{n+1} for the $(n+1)$th term, the formula for going from u_n to u_{n+1} is

$$u_n + 2 = u_{n+1}.$$

Sometimes we shall call this kind of formula an **iteration formula**.
It will usually be written with the $(n+1)$th term on the left-hand side, like this:

$$u_{n+1} = u_n + 2.$$

A2   The iteration formula of a sequence u is $u_{n+1} = u_n + 5$.
The first term, u_1, is 3.

Write down the values of u_2, u_3, u_4 and u_5.

A3   The iteration formula of a sequence v is $v_{n+1} = 1{\cdot}5v_n$.
The first term, v_1, is 40.

Write down the values of v_2, v_3, v_4 and v_5.

A4   Write down the first five terms of the sequence generated by each
of these iteration formulas. Start with $u_1 = 9$ each time.

(a) $u_{n+1} = 2u_n + 1$ (b) $u_{n+1} = \sqrt{u_n}$ (c) $u_{n+1} = 2(u_n + 1)$

A5   A sequence b has the iteration formula $b_{n+1} = \dfrac{b_n}{5} + 4$.

The first term, b_1, is 10. Calculate b_2, b_3, b_4 and b_5.

If the sequence in question A5 is continued, we get these values:

$b_6 = 5{\cdot}0016$ $b_7 = 5{\cdot}00032$ $b_8 = 5{\cdot}000064$ $b_9 = 5{\cdot}0000128$

The terms of the sequence get closer and closer to 5 as n increases.

We say this sequence **converges** towards 5, and we call 5 the **limit** of
the sequence.

A6   The iteration formula for a sequence c is $c_{n+1} = \dfrac{c_n}{2} + 3$.

The first term, c_1, is 8.

Calculate the values of c_2, c_3, c_4, . . . and so on, until you are
sure what limit the sequence approaches. Write down the limit.

A7   Do the same as in question A6 for the sequence d, where $d_1 = 6$

and the iteration formula is $d_{n+1} = \dfrac{d_n}{4} + 6$.

If we have a sequence which goes 5, 4·3, 4·14, 4·021, 4·0081, . . .
we would decide that its limit appears to be 4.

But suppose we have a sequence which goes like this:
   1·3, 0·94, 0·9247, 0·92324, 0·9232107, . . .

This sequence does not converge towards an obvious limit.
As the sequence goes on, the first decimal place 'settles down' to a constant
value 9, then the second decimal place settles down to 2, and so on.

If we want the limit **correct to 3 decimal places**, it would be 0.923,
because after a few terms nothing happens to change the first three places.

A8 A sequence s has the iteration formula $s_{n+1} = \dfrac{1}{s_n} + 5$.

The first term, s_1, is 2.

Calculate the values of $s_2, s_3, s_4, \ldots$ and so on, until you can say what the limit is, correct to 2 decimal places.

B Fixed points

Suppose that the iteration formula of a sequence is $p_{n+1} = \dfrac{p_n}{2} + 2$, and that $p_1 = 8$.

When we calculate p_2, p_3, etc. we get $p_2 = 6, \ p_3 = 5, \ p_4 = 4{\cdot}5, \ p_5 = 4{\cdot}25$.

We can use a set of arrow diagrams to show the sequence being generated.

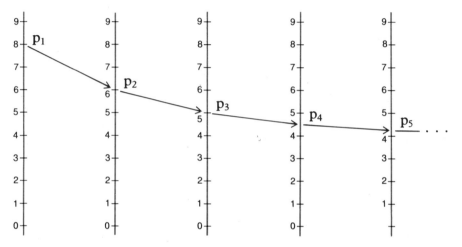

But it is more convenient to use a graph.

Each dot represents a term of the sequence.

The lines joining the dots do not mean anything. They are just there to help the eye.

We shall now investigate what happens when we use the same iteration formula, but different values of p_1.

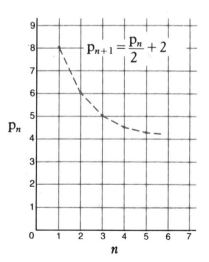

B1 The graph shows the sequence p, for

which $p_{n+1} = \dfrac{p_n}{2} + 2$, and $p_1 = 8$.

Copy the graph. Show on it also the sequences you get when you use the same iteration formula, but with p_1 equal to (a) 2 (b) 4

107

Here is a graph showing the sequences in question B1.

The iteration formula is the same for each one:

$$p_{n+1} = \frac{p_n}{2} + 2.$$

The values of p_1 for the three sequences are different.

Look at the sequence which starts with $p_1 = 4$.
When p_1 is 4, every term of the sequence is 4.
We say that 4 is a **fixed point** of the iteration

formula $p_{n+1} = \frac{p_n}{2} + 2.$

Look at the sequence which starts with $p_1 = 8$.
The terms of the sequence get closer and closer
to 4 as n increases.
This sequence converges towards 4, which is
the limit of the sequence.

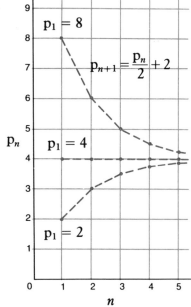

Look at the sequence which starts with $p_1 = 2$.
This sequence also converges towards 4.

B2 The iteration formula for a sequence q is $q_{n+1} = \frac{q_n}{3} + 2.$

   (a) Calculate the first six terms of the sequence q when $q_1 = 12$.

   (b) What number appears to be the limit of the sequence in part (a)?

   (c) Calculate the first six terms of the sequence q when $q_1 = 2$.
      Does this sequence converge to the same limit as before?

   (d) Take the value of the limit in parts (b) and (c) as the value of q_1.
      Calculate the first six terms of the sequence.
      What do you find?

B3 The iteration formula for a sequence r is $r_{n+1} = \frac{r_n + 8}{5}$

   (a) Calculate the first six terms of r when $r_1 = 32$.

   (b) What number appears to be the limit of the sequence?

   (c) Check that the limit is a fixed point of the iteration formula.

B4 The iteration formula for a sequence s is $s_{n+1} = \frac{1}{4}s_n + 12.$

   (a) Choose a value for s_1. Calculate the first six terms of the
      sequence and write down what its limit appears to be.

   (b) Check that the limit is a fixed point of the iteration formula.

So far we have had examples of sequences which converge towards a limit, and in every case the limit turns out to be a fixed point of the iteration formula.

This is a general fact about sequences, which we can state like this:

> If a sequence converges towards a limit, then that limit is a fixed point of the iteration formula for the sequence.

The reverse of this statement is **not** true. There are many examples of sequences which do **not** converge, but whose iteration formulas do have fixed points.

For example, suppose the iteration formula is $u_{n+1} = 2u_n - 3$.

If $u_1 = 4$, then we get $u_2 = 5$, $u_3 = 7$,
$u_4 = 11$, $u_5 = 19,. . .$

This sequence does **not** converge.

If $u_1 = 2$, then we get $u_2 = 1$, $u_3 = {}^-1$,
$u_4 = {}^-5$, $u_5 = {}^-13,. . .$

This sequence does not converge.

But if $u_1 = 3$, then we get $u_2 = 3$,
$u_3 = 3$, $u_4 = 3$, $u_5 = 3,. . .$

So 3 is a fixed point of the iteration formula.

These three sequences are shown in the graph on the right.

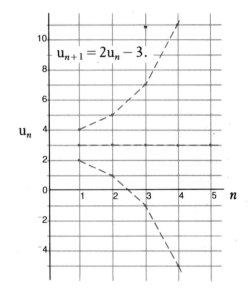

B5 The iteration formula of a sequence t is $t_{n+1} = 3t_n - 4$.

(a) Calculate the first six terms of the sequence when $t_1 = 5$. Does this sequence converge?

(b) Calculate the first six terms when $t_1 = 1$. Does this sequence converge?

(c) The formula $t_{n+1} = 3t_n - 4$ does have a fixed point, which is a simple whole number. Find out what it is.

B6 A sequence s has the iteration formula $s_{n+1} = \sqrt{(1 - s_n)}$.
Let $s_1 = 0 \cdot 5$. Calculate the first 10 terms of the sequence.
(If your calculator has a 'change sign' key $\boxed{+/-}$, a good way to do $1 - s_n$ is $s_n \boxed{+/-} \boxed{+} \boxed{1} \boxed{=}$.)

The sequence converges towards a limit whose value to 3 d.p. is $0 \cdot 618$. The terms are alternately above and below the limit. Check that $0 \cdot 618$ is, approximately, a fixed point of the iteration formula.

109

C Iteration formulas with more than one fixed point

The iteration formula for a sequence v is $v_{n+1} = \dfrac{2}{v_n + 1}$.

When you have to use an iteration formula, it is worth spending a few moments deciding how you can best use your calculator. You want to avoid having to key in long strings of digits.

One way to do $\dfrac{2}{v_n + 1}$ is to use the **reciprocal key** $\boxed{\frac{1}{x}}$.

You do $\dfrac{v_n + 1}{2}$ first and then 'invert' it by using $\boxed{\frac{1}{x}}$.

One possible key sequence for the formula is given here. (You will have to check that it works on your calculator.)

Enter the value of v_1 $\boxed{+}\,\boxed{1}\,\boxed{=}\,\boxed{\div}\,\boxed{2}\,\boxed{=}\,\boxed{\frac{1}{x}}$

C1   Copy the table below.
Calculate the first 8 terms of the sequence v whose iteration formula is given above, for the different first terms given in the table.

Enter the results in your table (to 3 d.p.) and describe the behaviour of each sequence.
(This can be done as a group activity, with different people doing different sequences.)

v_1	v_2	v_3	v_4	v_5	v_6	v_7	v_8	Behaviour
3	0·5	1·333	0·857	1·077	0·963	1·019	0·991	Converges towards 1
2								
1								
0								
⁻1								
⁻2								
⁻3								
⁻4								

C2   Try some more values for v_1. See if you can get a sequence which converges towards a limit of ⁻2 (one of the fixed points of the iteration formula.)

C3   The iteration formula $w_{n+1} = w_n^2$ has two fixed points which are both easy to spot. What are they?
Investigate the behaviour of the sequence w when w_1 is
(a) greater than 1   (b) between 0 and 1   (c) less than 0

110

D Fixed points and equations

D1 (a) Use the iteration formula $u_{n+1} = \dfrac{u_n + 8}{3}$ to generate

a sequence starting with $u_1 = 6$. Calculate enough terms to be sure of the limit of the sequence.

(b) Check that the value you get for the limit in (a) is a fixed point of the iteration formula.

In question D1 you found a fixed point of the iteration formula $u_{n+1} = \dfrac{u_n + 8}{3}$

by generating a sequence which converged to a limit. The limit is a fixed point of the iteration formula.

Another way to find the fixed point is as follows.

Let the fixed point be x.
Then if u_1 is x, then $u_2, u_3, u_4, \ldots$ will all be x. In other words, every term of the sequence will be equal to x.

So replace both u_n and u_{n+1} in the formula by x.

We get an equation, which we shall call the **fixed point equation** of the iteration formula. It is

$$x = \frac{x + 8}{3}$$

By solving this equation we find the fixed point.

Multiply both sides by 3. $3x = x + 8$
Subtract x from both sides. $2x = 8$
$$x = 4$$

So the fixed point of the iteration formula is 4, as you found by the other method.

D2 (a) Calculate the fixed point of the iteration formula $u_{n+1} = \dfrac{u_n + 18}{4}$

by solving the equation $x = \dfrac{x + 18}{4}$.

(b) Use the iteration formula to generate a sequence starting with $u_1 = 10$. Does the sequence converge? If so, check that its limit is equal to the fixed point.

D3 By solving equations, find the fixed points of these iteration formulas.

(a) $u_{n+1} = \dfrac{u_n + 15}{6}$ (b) $u_{n+1} = \dfrac{u_n + 5}{3}$ (c) $u_{n+1} = \frac{1}{2} u_n + 7$

(d) $u_{n+1} = \frac{1}{3} u_n + 6$ (e) $u_{n+1} = \dfrac{u_n - 2}{3}$ (f) $u_{n+1} = 3u_n - 4$

Worked example

Find the fixed point of the iteration formula $u_{n+1} = \dfrac{6}{u_n + 1}$.

Let the fixed point be x. As before, replace u_n and u_{n+1} both by x.

$$x = \frac{6}{x+1}$$

Multiply both sides by $x+1$. $\quad\quad\quad x(x+1) = 6$

Multiply out brackets. $\quad\quad\quad\quad\quad x^2 + x = 6$

Subtract 6 from both sides. $\quad\quad\quad x^2 + x - 6 = 0$

Now we have a quadratic equation to solve.
The left-hand side can be factorised.

$$(x+3)(x-2) = 0$$

So either $x + 3 = 0$ or $x - 2 = 0$.

So $\quad\quad\quad x = {}^-3$ or $\quad\quad x = 2$.

There are **two** fixed points, $^-3$ and 2.

D4 Check that both $^-3$ and 2 are fixed points of $u_{n+1} = \dfrac{6}{u_n + 1}$.

D5 Calculate the fixed points of the iteration formula $u_{n+1} = \dfrac{15}{u_n + 2}$.

Check each one.

D6 Calculate the fixed points of the iteration formula $u_{n+1} = \dfrac{18}{u_n - 7}$.

D7 Calculate the fixed points of each of these iteration formulas.

(a) $u_{n+1} = \dfrac{16}{u_n + 6}$ (b) $u_{n+1} = \dfrac{21}{4 + u_n}$ (c) $u_{n+1} = \dfrac{6}{5 - u_n}$

E   Solving equations by iteration (1)

We have seen that there are two methods of finding the fixed point(s)
of an iteration formula.

Method 1 Generate a converging sequence. The limit of the sequence
is a fixed point of the iteration formula.

Method 2 Write the equation for the fixed points. Solve it by algebra.

Equations are often very difficult or impossible to solve by algebra.
But it is sometimes possible to use an iteration formula to solve an equation
which we cannot solve by algebra. An example will explain the method.

Suppose we start with the equation $x = \dfrac{4}{x+1}$, and we are not able to solve it by algebra.

We can think of this equation as the fixed point equation of the iteration formula $u_{n+1} = \dfrac{4}{u_n + 1}$.

Now we use **method 1** to find a fixed point of this iteration formula. We choose a value for u_1. Suppose $u_1 = 1$. Then we get

u_1	u_2	u_3	u_4	u_5	u_6	u_7
1	2	1·333...	1·714...	1·473...	1·617...	1·528...

u_8	u_9	u_{10}	u_{11}	u_{12}	u_{13}
1·581...	1·549...	1·569...	1·556...	1·564...	1·559...

This sequence appears to converge towards a limit which, correct to 2 decimal places, is 1·56.

This limit is a fixed point of the iteration formula $u_{n+1} = \dfrac{4}{u_n + 1}$, and so it is a solution of $x = \dfrac{4}{x+1}$.

(Check: When $x = 1·56$, then $\dfrac{4}{x+1} = \dfrac{4}{2·56} = 1·5625$.)

E1   The equation $x = \dfrac{1}{x} + 2$ can be thought of as the

fixed point equationof the iteration formula $u_{n+1} = \dfrac{1}{u_n} + 2$.

  (a) Use this iteration formula to generate a sequence starting with $u_1 = 2$. Continue until you can write down the limit correct to 2 decimal places.

  (b) Check that the limit approximately satisfies the equation $x = \dfrac{1}{x} + 2$.

E2   The equation $x = \dfrac{5}{x + 3}$ can be thought of as the fixed point

equation of an iteration formula.

  (a) Write down the iteration formula, in the form $u_{n+1} = \ldots$

  (b) Use this iteration formula to generate a sequence, starting with $u_1 = 1$. Find the limit correct to 1 decimal place.

    (A suitable key sequence for the iteration is

$$u_n \rightarrow \boxed{+}\,\boxed{3}\,\boxed{=}\,\boxed{\div}\,\boxed{5}\,\boxed{=}\,\boxed{\tfrac{1}{x}} \rightarrow u_{n+1}.)$$

  (c) Check that the limit approximately satisfies the equation $x = \dfrac{5}{x + 3}$.

Going from an equation to an iteration formula

If we are trying to solve the equation $x = \dfrac{5}{x+3}$, we can use the iteration

formula $u_{n+1} = \dfrac{5}{u_n + 3}$.

It is easy to write down the iteration formula because the original equation is in the form

$$x = \text{an expression containing } x$$

We simply replace the x on the left-hand side by u_{n+1}, and the x in the expression on the right-hand side by u_n.

If we want to solve an equation which is not in the form above, we first have to re-arrange it into this form.

For example, suppose we want to solve the equation $x(x+1) = 6$.

We can re-arrange it by dividing both sides by $x + 1$.

This gives us $x = \dfrac{6}{x+1}$, and the iteration formula is $u_{n+1} = \dfrac{6}{u_n + 1}$.

E3 (a) Re-arrange the equation $x(x+2) = 10$ into the form 'x = an expression containing x'.

(b) Write down the corresponding iteration formula.

(c) Use the iteration formula to generate a sequence, starting with $u_1 = 3$. Continue until you can write down the limit correct to 1 decimal place.

(d) Check that the limit approximately satisfies the equation $x(x+2) =$

E4 Repeat question E3 for the equation $x(x+3) = 20$.

Sometimes it may take several steps of working to re-arrange an equation in the form 'x = an expression containing x'.

Worked example

Re-arrange the equation $x^2 + 2x - 5 = 0$ in the form 'x = an expression containing x'. Write down an iteration formula and use it to find a solution of the equation, correct to 1 decimal place.

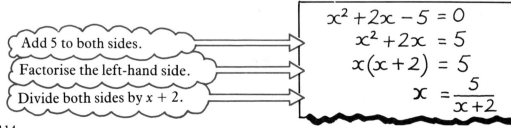

Add 5 to both sides.

Factorise the left-hand side.

Divide both sides by $x + 2$.

$$x^2 + 2x - 5 = 0$$
$$x^2 + 2x = 5$$
$$x(x+2) = 5$$
$$x = \dfrac{5}{x+2}$$

From this re-arrangement we get the iteration formula $u_{n+1} = \dfrac{5}{u_n + 2}$.

E5 Use the iteration formula above, starting with $u_1 = 1$, to generate a sequence. Find the limit correct to 2 d.p. Check that the limit approximately satisfies the equation $x^2 + 2x - 5 = 0$.

E6 (a) Show that the equation $x^2 + 5x = 10$ can be written in the

form $x = \dfrac{10}{x + 5}$.

(b) Write down the corresponding iteration formula.

(c) Starting with a first term of 1, generate the sequence and find its limit, correct to 2 decimal places.

(d) Check that the limit approximately satisfies the equation $x^2 + 5x = 10$.

E7 (a) Show that the equation $x^2 - 3x - 5 = 0$ can be written in

the form $x = \dfrac{5}{x - 3}$.

(b) Write down the corresponding iteration formula.

(c) Use the iteration formula to generate a sequence, starting with a first term of 5. At first it looks as though the sequence will not converge to a limit, but eventually it does converge. Find the limit, correct to 2 decimal places.

(d) Check that the limit approximately satisfies the equation $x^2 - 3x - 5 = 0$.

F Solving equations by iteration (2)

Not every way of re-writing an equation in the form $x = \ldots$ leads to a suitable iteration formula.

The next question gives an example where the iteration formula is no use for solving the equation.

F1 (a) Show that the equation $x^2 + x - 5 = 0$ can be re-written in the form $x = 5 - x^2$.

(b) The corresponding iteration formula is $u_{n+1} = 5 - u_n^2$.

Choose a value for u_1 and generate the sequence. What happens?

Is it different if you use a different starting value?

Snags in the iterative method of solving equations

In question F1, the equation $x^2 + x - 5 = 0$ was re-arranged as $x = 5 - x^2$. This led to the iteration formula $u_{n+1} = 5 - u_n^2$. But this formula does not give a converging sequence, so it is no use for solving the equation. We would need to try a different re-arrangement of the equation, for example $x = \dfrac{5}{x + 1}$.

Another problem arises when an equation has more than one solution. An iteration formula may lead to one of the solutions but not to the other. You may need to use a different formula to get the other solution.

F2   The cube root of 10 is the value of x such that $x^3 = 10$.
So we can find the cube root of 10 by solving $x^3 = 10$.
Here are two different ways of re-arranging $x^3 = 10$.

Divide both sides by x.	$x^3 = 10$ $x^2 = \dfrac{10}{x}$
Take the square root of both sides.	$x = \sqrt{\left(\dfrac{10}{x}\right)}$

	$x^3 = 10$
Divide both sides by x^2.	$x = \dfrac{10}{x^2}$

From these re-arrangements we get these iteration formulas.

$$(1)\ \ u_{n+1} = \sqrt{\left(\frac{10}{u_n}\right)} \qquad (2)\ \ u_{n+1} = \frac{10}{u_n^2}$$

It is a good idea to start the iteration by choosing a value of u_1 which is itself a fairly good approximation to the solution. We know that the cube root of 10 is a bit larger than 2, because $2^3 = 8$, so 2 is a good value to start with.

(a) Let $u_1 = 2$. Use iteration formula (1) to generate a sequence. Continue until you can give the solution correct to 2 d.p.

(b) Use formula (2) starting with $u_1 = 2$ and see what happens.

F3   Here is another way of re-arranging $x^3 = 10$.

$$\begin{aligned} &x^3 = 10 \\ \text{Multiply both sides by } x. \quad &x^4 = 10x \\ \text{Take the square root of both sides.} \quad &x^2 = \sqrt{(10x)} \\ \text{Take the square root of both sides again.} \quad &x = \sqrt{(\sqrt{(10x)})} \\ \text{From this we get the iteration formula} \quad &u_{n+1} = \sqrt{(\sqrt{(10u_n)})} \end{aligned}$$

Use this formula starting with $u_1 = 2$ to find the solution of the equation, correct to 2 d.p. You should find that the sequence converges more quickly than the sequence you got using $u_{n+1} = \sqrt{\left(\dfrac{10}{u_n}\right)}$.

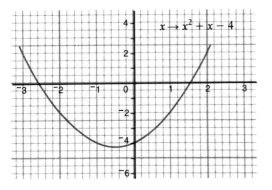

F4 The graph of the function

$$x \to x^2 + x - 4$$

shows that there is a solution of the equation $x^2 + x - 4 = 0$ close to 1·6 and another close to $^-$2·6.

Here are two different ways of re-arranging $x^2 + x - 4 = 0$.

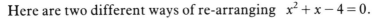

Add 4 to both sides.
Factorise.

$$x^2 + x - 4 = 0$$
$$x^2 + x = 4$$
$$x(x + 1) = 4$$

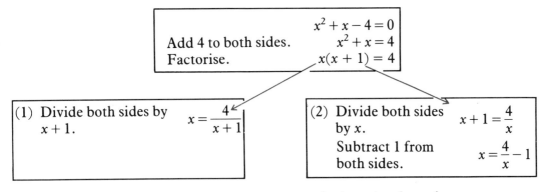

(1) Divide both sides by $x + 1$.

$$x = \frac{4}{x + 1}$$

(2) Divide both sides by x.
Subtract 1 from both sides.

$$x + 1 = \frac{4}{x}$$
$$x = \frac{4}{x} - 1$$

From these re-arrangements, we get the iteration formulas

$$(1) \ u_{n+1} = \frac{4}{u_n + 1} \qquad (2) \ u_{n+1} = \frac{4}{u_n} - 1$$

(a) Let u_1 be 1·6.
Use each of the two iteration formulas to generate a sequence. Do both sequences converge to limits? Or only one?

Find correct to 2 d.p. the solution of $x^2 + x - 4 = 0$ which is close to 1·6.

(b) The other solution is close to $^-$2·6. Let u_1 be $^-$2·6.
Once again, use each of the two iteration formulas to generate a sequence. Which one converges to a limit this time?

Find the solution correct to 2 d.p.

F5 The equation $x(x + 2) = 5$ has a solution close to 1·5 and another close to $^-$3·5.

Use iteration formulas to find both solutions correct to 2 d.p.

F6 Use iteration formulas to find both solutions of the equation $x^2 + 4x - 9 = 0$. First draw a graph of $x \to x^2 + 4x - 9$ in order to locate the solutions approximately.

117

A Saving

When you pay money into a bank 'deposit account' (or a building society) it earns interest. The bank pays you for being able to use your money. The bank lends the money to other people or businesses, who pay the bank even more interest than the bank pays you, and in that way the bank covers its costs and makes a profit.

You may wonder why you can't lend your money directly to the other people or businesses, and get the higher interest rate yourself. You can do, but it is usually a more risky affair. If the business goes bankrupt, you lose your money. Banks lend to many different companies and can afford to take the occasional risk.

Banks and building societies have various savings schemes, each with its **annual interest rate**.

Suppose you invest £500 in a building society, and the interest rate is 8% p.a. (p.a. = per annum, or per year).

After 1 year the amount invested is multiplied by **1·08**.
So after 1 year the amount is £500 × 1·08 = £540.

After 1 more year, the amount is multiplied by 1·08 again,
so after 2 years it is £540 × 1·08 = £583·20, and so on.

> **A1** Dawn invests £80 in a bank deposit account. The interest rate is 6% p.a. Calculate the amount in Dawn's account after 3 years, to the nearest penny.

Jim invests £5000 in a bank. The interest rate is 8% p.a.
If Jim leaves the money in the bank for 1 year, the amount would be £5000 × 1·08 = £5400.

Jim decides to leave his £5000 in the bank for six months only.
You might think the bank should pay half the yearly rate of interest, that is 4% for six months. Suppose the bank does this.

After six month's Jim's amount is £5000 × 1·04 = £5200.	After another six months, his amount is £5200 × 1·04 = **£5408**.
Suppose Jim now decides to leave his money in the bank for another six months.	But this is more than Jim would have got by leaving his money in for 1 year at 8% per year!

The reason for the discrepancy is this: an increase of 4% followed by another increase of 4% is **not** equivalent to an increase of 8%.

This is because multiplying by $1 \cdot 04$ and then by $1 \cdot 04$ again is equivalent to multiplying by $1 \cdot 04 \times 1 \cdot 04$, or $1 \cdot 0816$, and this means an increase of **8·16%**, not 8%.

If the yearly interest rate is 8%, the six-monthly rate has to be $3 \cdot 923\%$, because

$$1 \cdot 039\,23 \times 1 \cdot 039\,23 = 1 \cdot 08.$$

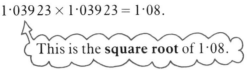

This is the **square root** of $1 \cdot 08$.

A2   Calculate the **three-monthly rate**, when the yearly rate is 8%.

B   Borrowing

Suppose you want to buy something expensive. You may decide to borrow the money from a bank. The bank will charge you interest on the loan. The higher the rate of interest, the costlier is the loan.

A simple kind of loan is one which is made for a fixed period, and where the borrower repays the full amount, including interest, at the end of the period.

For example, suppose Anar borrows £500 for 4 years, and the interest rate is 20% p.a.

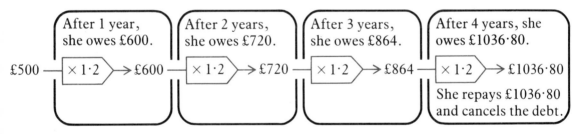

After 1 year, she owes £600.
After 2 years, she owes £720.
After 3 years, she owes £864.
After 4 years, she owes £1036·80.

£500 —|× 1·2|→ £600 —|× 1·2|→ £720 —|× 1·2|→ £864 —|× 1·2|→ £1036·80

She repays £1036·80 and cancels the debt.

A more common way to repay a loan is by **instalments**.
Suppose John borrows £100. The interest rate is 15% p.a. He agrees to repay £30 at the end of each year until the debt is cancelled.

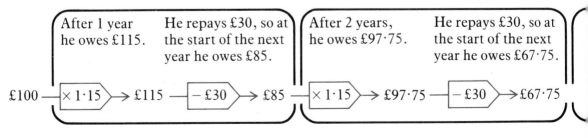

After 1 year he owes £115.   He repays £30, so at the start of the next year he owes £85.
After 2 years, he owes £97·75.   He repays £30, so at the start of the next year he owes £67·75.

£100 —|× 1·15|→ £115 —|− £30|→ £85 —|× 1·15|→ £97·75 —|− £30|→ £67·75

B1   Continue the calculation above and find out how many years it takes John to repay the loan.

119

In the previous question, you were given the interest rate and the size of the instalments and were asked to find out how long it would take to repay the loan.

In practice we start from the interest rate and the time to full repayment, and calculate the size of the instalments.

Worked example

Karl borrows £400. The interest rate is 20% p.a.
He agrees to repay in two equal instalments, one after 1 year and the other after 2 years. Calculate the instalment.

Let each instalment be £I.

After 1 year, Karl owes £400 × 1·2 = £480.
He then repays £I, so at the start of the next year he owes £$(480 - I)$.

After 2 years, Karl owes £$(480 - I) \times 1\cdot2$
$$= £(480 \times 1\cdot2 \; - \; I \times 1\cdot2)$$
$$= £(576 - 1\cdot2I)$$

He then repays £I and cancels the debt. So

$$576 - 1\cdot2I - I = 0$$
$$576 - 2\cdot2I = 0$$
$$576 = 2\cdot2I$$

$$\frac{576}{2\cdot2} = I$$

$$I = 261\cdot82 \text{ (to 2 d.p.)}$$

So Karl pays two yearly instalments of **£261·82**.

B2 Rowena borrows £1000. The interest rate is 24%.
She agrees to repay in two equal yearly instalments.
Calculate the instalments.

B3 Sam borrows £1000. The interest rate is 20%. He agrees to repay in three equal yearly instalments of £I.

(a) Show that after 2 years, just before the second instalment is paid, Sam owes £$(1440 - 1\cdot2I)$.

(b) Write down an expression for the amount Sam owes just after the second instalment is paid.

(c) Show that after 3 years, just before the third instalment is paid, Sam owes £$(1728 - 2\cdot64I)$.

(d) The third instalment cancels the debt. Write an equation which says this and solve it to find the value of I.

Most personal loans are repaid in monthly instalments.
When people buy things on **hire purchase** they are being given a loan by a
hire purchase company. The repayments are usually monthly.

The interest rate for loans is usually called the **annual percentage rate** (APR).
The table below shows the size of monthly instalments when £100 is borrowed
at various different APRs.

Time to full repayment

		1 year	2 years	3 years	4 years	5 years
	20%	£9·19	£5·01	£3·63	£2·96	£2·56
	22%	£9·27	£5·09	£3·72	£3·05	£2·65
APR	24%	£9·35	£5·17	£3·80	£3·13	£2·75
	26%	£9·42	£5·25	£3·89	£3·22	£2·84
	28%	£9·50	£5·33	£3·97	£3·31	£2·93
	30%	£9·58	£5·41	£4·06	£3·40	£3·03

To find the monthly instalments for loans of amounts other than £100,
you scale up or down.
For example, the instalments for a loan of £250 are 2·5 times those for a loan of £100.

B4 What are the monthly instalments for a loan of £850 at
APR 24% repaid over 3 years?

B5 What are the monthly instalments for a loan of £80 at APR 28%
repaid over 2 years?

The table can be used to find (approximately) the annual percentage rate of
interest when you are told the monthly instalments and the repayment period.

B6 A company offers a loan of £500, to be repaid in monthly
instalments of £15·30 over a period of 4 years.

(a) What would the monthly instalments be if the loan were
£100 instead of £500?
(b) Use the table above to find the APR, approximately.

B7 The cash price of a car is £3500. If you pay £500 now you
can have a loan to cover the rest of the price. The loan is to
be repaid in 36 monthly instalments of £117. Find the APR.

B8 Which of these loans has the lower APR?
A: a loan of £800 repaid in 24 monthly instalments of £42
B: a loan of £800 repaid in 36 monthly instalments of £30·40

Companies offering loans are legally required to state the APR.
This enables the would-be borrower to compare the costs of loans.

10 The sine and cosine functions (2)

A Amplitude and period

The graph of the function $\theta \to \sin \theta$ has a 'wave' shape. (In fact the graph is often called a 'sine wave'.) The period of the graph is 360°.

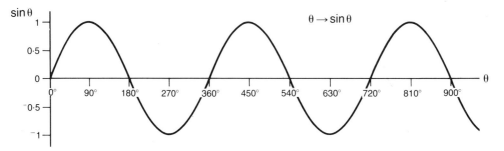

By making slight alterations to the function, we can modify the graph without altering the overall 'wave' shape.

The graph of $\theta \to \sin \theta$ oscillates between a maximum value of 1 and a minimum value of $^-1$.
1 is called the **amplitude** of the wave.

We can alter the amplitude by multiplying $\sin \theta$ by a number, for example 1·5. This gives us the function $\theta \to 1\cdot5 \sin \theta$, whose graph looks like this. The amplitude is 1·5. (The period is still 360°.)

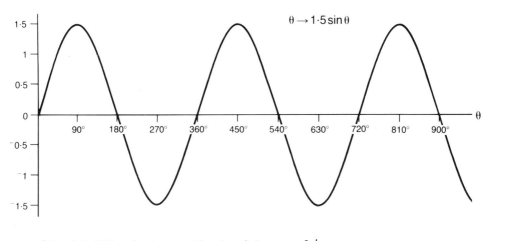

A1 (a) What is the amplitude of the sine wave shown on the right?

(b) Write down the function in the form $\theta \to \ldots$

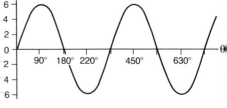

Another way to vary the graph is to replace sin θ by sin 2θ, sin 3θ, etc.

'sin 2θ' means 'the sine of twice θ'.
So if θ is, say, 30°, then 2θ is 60° and sin 2θ is sin 60°, or **0·866...**

A2 Draw axes with θ from 0° to 360°.

(a) Calculate the value of sin θ when θ is 0°, 30°, 60°, 90°, . . . up to 360° and draw the graph of θ → sin θ.

(b) Copy and complete this table of values for the function θ → sin 2θ. (Work to 2 d.p.)

θ	0°	30°	60°	90°	120°	. . . up to 360°
sin 2θ	0	0·87				

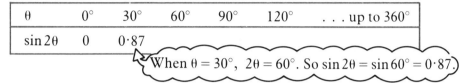

When θ = 30°, 2θ = 60°. So sin 2θ = sin 60° = 0·87.

(c) Draw the graph of θ → sin 2θ on the same axes as before. What is the period of the graph?

We can work out the period of the function θ → sin 2θ without actually drawing the graph.

We know that the ordinary sine graph repeats itself after 360°.
So the graph of θ → sin 2θ will repeat itself when 2θ reaches 360°.
In other words it will repeat itself when θ reaches 180°.
So its period is **180°**.

We can alter the amplitude by multiplying sin 2θ by a number.
Here, for example, is the graph of θ → 4 sin 2θ, with amplitude 4.

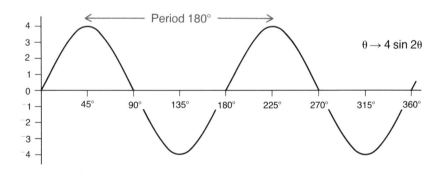

A3 (a) The graph of θ → sin 3θ will repeat itself when 3θ reaches 360°. What is the period of the graph of θ → sin 3θ?

(b) What is the amplitude of the graph of θ → 4 sin 3θ?

A4 Write down the amplitude and the period of the graph of each of these functions.

(a) θ → 5 sin 2θ   (b) θ → 10 sin 3θ   (c) θ → 20 sin (½θ)

123

B The length of day

This table shows the length of day (sunrise to sunset) in Newcastle,
every ten days during a typical year.

Date	n (day number)	L (length in hours)	Date	n (day number)	L (length in hours)
10 Jan	10	7·6	9 July	190	17·1
20 Jan	20	8·0	19 July	200	16·7
30 Jan	30	8·6	29 July	210	16·1
9 Feb	40	9·3	8 Aug	220	15·5
19 Feb	50	10·0	18 Aug	230	14·8
1 Mar	60	10·7	28 Aug	240	14·1
11 Mar	70	11·5	7 Sept	250	13·4
21 Mar	80	12·2	17 Sept	260	12·7
31 Mar	90	12·9	27 Sept	270	11·9
10 Apr	100	13·7	7 Oct	280	11·2
20 Apr	110	14·4	17 Oct	290	10·5
30 Apr	120	15·1	27 Oct	300	9·7
10 May	130	15·8	6 Nov	310	9·1
20 May	140	16·4	16 Nov	320	8·4
30 May	150	16·9	26 Nov	330	7·9
9 June	160	17·2	6 Dec	340	7·5
19 June	170	17·4	16 Dec	350	7·2
29 June	180	17·3	26 Dec	360	7·3

B1 The graph below was drawn from the information in the table.
A school in Newcastle plans a sponsored walk on 15 April. Estimate
the length of the day on 15 April, using either the graph or the table.

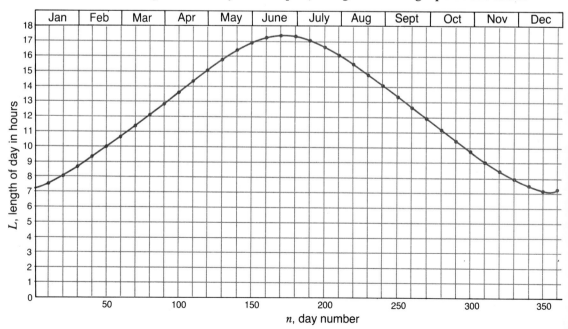

124

B2 Estimate each of these.
   (a) Which is the longest day? (Estimate its date.)
   (b) Which is the shortest day?
   (c) When is the day 12 hours long? (Estimate the dates.)

B3 (a) How much longer is the day on 9 February than on 30 January?
   (b) How much longer is the day on 30 April than on 20 April?
   (c) In what part of the year are the days lengthening fastest?
   (d) When are they shortening fastest?

The graph looks similar in shape to a sine curve, but it does not drop below the horizontal axis.

In fact there is a formula with a sine in it which fits the curve quite well. It is
$$L = 12 \cdot 3 + 5 \sin (0 \cdot 986n - 80 \cdot 8)$$

n stands for the number of the day, and L for the length of that day in hours (in Newcastle).

B4 The formula is only approximately true. It is less accurate than the table. Use the formula to find the length of day on these dates, and compare your result with the table.

   (a) 9 February (n is 40. Start by calculating $0 \cdot 986n - 80 \cdot 8$, find the sine of this, multiply by 5 and then add $12 \cdot 3$.)

   (b) 31 March   (c) 8 August   (d) 6 December

The length of day on any given date depends on the **latitude** of the place where you are.
If you know the length of day in Newcastle, you can find the length of day in other places in the British Isles by using this formula:
$$L' = (0 \cdot 04\lambda - 1 \cdot 2)L + 26 \cdot 4 - 0 \cdot 48\lambda$$

L' stands for the length of day at the place you are interested in.
λ (the Greek letter l, called 'lambda') stands for the latitude of the place.
L stands for the length of day in Newcastle.

This formula too is only approximately true. It is reasonably accurate for latitudes between 50°N and 60°N. Outside this range it is inaccurate.

B5 (a) Use the table to find the length of day in Newcastle on 16 November.
   (b) Use the formula for L' to find the length of day in Bristol on 16 November. The latitude of Bristol is $51 \cdot 5°$N.

B6 Use the first formula on this page to find the length of day in Newcastle on your birthday. Estimate from an atlas the latitude of your home (to the nearest $0 \cdot 1°$) and use the second formula to find the length of day at home on your birthday.

11 Inequalities

A Regions

When we use x- and y-coordinates to
describe the positions of points in a
plane, then **lines** can be described by
equations.

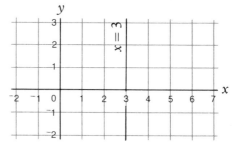

The line shown in the diagram has
the equation $x = 3$.

The line $x = 3$ is the boundary between two **regions**, one either side
of the line.
Every point in the left-hand region has an x-coordinate which is
less than 3. Every point in the right-hand region has an x-coordinate
which is greater than 3.

We can describe the two regions by
inequalities.

To the left of the line is the region $x < 3$.

To the right of the line is the region $x > 3$.

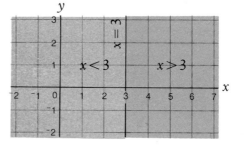

A1 Write down an inequality which describes each **unshaded** region.

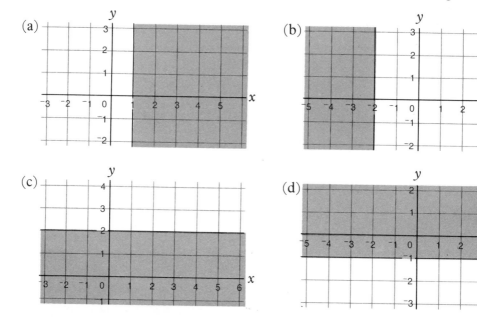

(a)

(b)

(c)

(d)

Think about the expression $2x + 3y$.
If you say what the values of x and y are to be, then the value
of $2x + 3y$ can be calculated.
So what we have is a **function** of x and y, which we can write as

$$(x, y) \rightarrow 2x + 3y.$$

For example, when $(x, y) = (4, 1)$, then $2x + 3y = 8 + 3 = 11$.

The red numbers in the diagram below show the value of $2x + 3y$ at
various points.

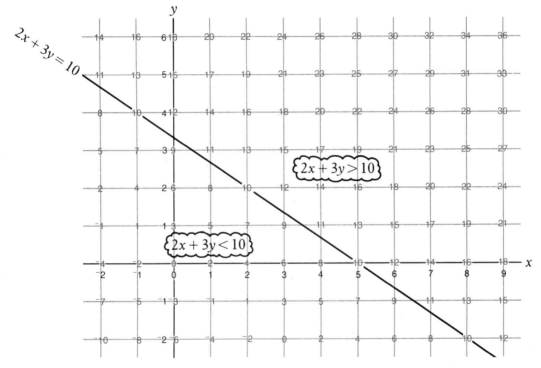

The sloping line goes through all the points for which $2x + 3y = 10$, so its
equation is $2x + 3y = 10$.

The line $2x + 3y = 10$ separates the plane into two regions.
At every point in the region **above** the line, the value of $2x + 3y$ is greater than 10.

So we can describe the region above the line as the region $2x + 3y > 10$.

Similarly, the region below the line is the region $2x + 3y < 10$.

A2 Calculate the value of $2x + 3y$ at each of these points and
say whether they are in the region $2x + 3y > 10$ or the region
$2x + 3y < 10$, or on the line $2x + 3y = 10$.

(a) $(4 \cdot 5, 0 \cdot 5)$ (b) $(3 \cdot 5, 1)$ (c) $(9 \cdot 5, {}^{-}2 \cdot 5)$

(d) $({}^{-}3 \cdot 5, 5 \cdot 5)$ (e) $(2 \cdot 6, 1 \cdot 5)$

Now check from the diagram where possible.

It is not always true that the inequality with '>' describes the region above a line, and the inequality with '<' the region below the line.

The red numbers on this diagram show the value of $x - y$ at various points.

For example, at the point $(3, 2)$ the value of $x - y = 3 - 2 = 1$.

The sloping line has the equation $x - y = 3$.

You can see from the diagram that at every point **above** the line, $x - y$ is less than 3, and at every point **below** the line, $x - y$ is greater than 3.

So **above** the line is the region $x - y < 3$, and **below** the line is the region $x - y > 3$.

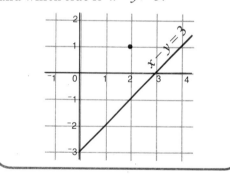

Suppose that all you are given is the line $x - y = 3$. You do not know which side of the line is the region $x - y < 3$, and which side is $x - y > 3$.

All you need to do is to test **one** point which is not on the line itself.

For example, take the point $(2, 1)$, which is **above** the line.

Does $(2, 1)$ satisfy $x - y < 3$ or $x - y > 3$?

It satisfies $x - y < 3$, because $2 - 1 = 1$, which is less than 3.

So above the line is the region $x - y < 3$, (and below is $x - y > 3$).

A3 Write down an inequality which describes each **unshaded** region. (Use the 'test point' method described above.)

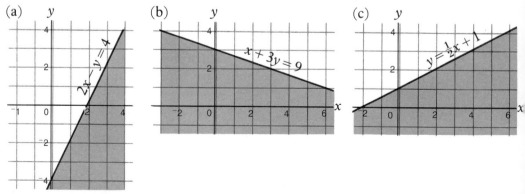

(a) $2x - y = 4$

(b) $x + 3y = 9$

(c) $y = \frac{1}{2}x + 1$

Drawing regions

We show a region in a drawing by shading out the part of the plane which does **not** belong to it.

Worked example

Draw the region $3x + 4y > 18$.

First draw the line $3x + 4y = 18$.

The easiest way to do this is to find where the line crosses the axes.

When $x = 0$, $4y = 18$, so $y = 4\frac{1}{2}$.   When $y = 0$, $3x = 18$, so $x = 6$.

After drawing the line $3x + 4y = 18$, choose a 'test point' not on it, for example $(2, 1)$.

At $(2, 1)$ the value of $3x + 4y$ is $6 + 4 = 10$. So $(2, 1)$ is in the region $3x + 4y < 18$.

So the region $3x + 4y > 18$ is **above** the line.

So shade out the part of the plane **below** the line.

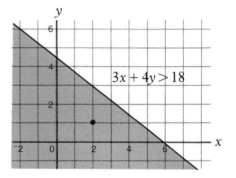

A4   Draw the region $2x + y < 6$.

A5   Draw each of the following regions on separate diagrams.

(a) $2x - y > 5$ (b) $x - 3y < 6$ (c) $x - y > {}^-3$ (d) $y < 2x$

A region may have a curve as a boundary. If the equation of the curve is in the form '$y =$ a function of x', then it is easy to write down inequalities for the regions above and below the curve.

For example, this diagram shows the curve whose equation is $y = x^2 + 1$.

For any given value of x, the point where $y = x^2 + 1$ lies on the curve. At points above the curve, the value of y will be greater than $x^2 + 1$, and at points below the curve, y will be less than $x^2 + 1$.

So **above** the curve is the region $y > x^2 + 1$.

And **below** the curve is the region $y < x^2 + 1$.

(The same idea also works for a straight line, when its equation is in the form '$y = \ldots$'.)

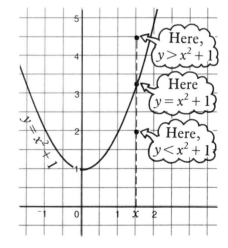

A6   Draw the graph of $y = x(4 - x)$ for values of x from ${}^-1$ to 5.
On the diagram show the region $y < x(4 - x)$.

B Regions with two boundaries

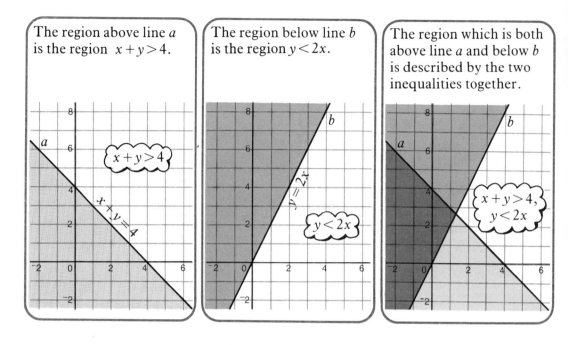

The region above line a is the region $x+y>4$.

The region below line b is the region $y<2x$.

The region which is both above line a and below b is described by the two inequalities together.

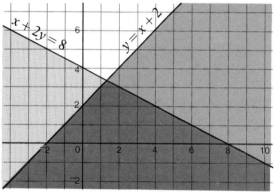

B1 Choose a test point somewhere inside the unshaded region in the diagram on the left.

(a) Does your test point satisfy $x+2y<8$ **or** $x+2y>8$?

(b) Does your test point satisfy $y<x+2$ **or** $y>x+2$?

(c) Write down the pair of inequalities which describe the unshaded region

B2 Write down a pair of inequalities which describes each unshaded region.

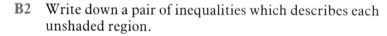

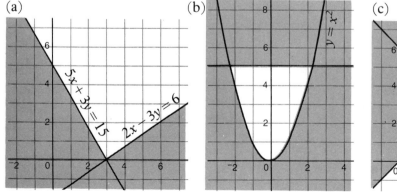
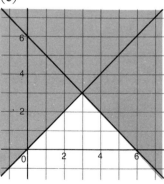

(a)

(b)

(c)

130

Worked example

Draw the region described by the inequalities $x - 2y > 4$, $x + 3y > 6$.

1 Draw the line $x - 2y = 4$.

Use a test point to decide which side of the line is $x - 2y < 4$ and which is $x - 2y > 4$.

Shade out the part you do not want, leaving the region $x - 2y > 4$.

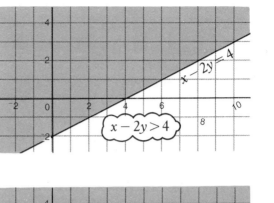

2 Draw the line $x + 3y = 6$.

Use a test point to decide which side of the line is which.

Shade out the part you do not want. (Some will be shaded already.)

The region left unshaded satisfies both inequalities $x - 2y > 4$ and $x + 3y > 6$.

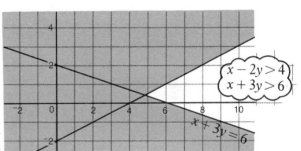

B3 Draw the region described by the two inequalities $x + y < 5$ and $y > x$.

B4 Draw the region described by the two inequalities $x + 2y > 8$ and $y < 5$.

B5 Draw the region described by the two inequalities $x - y < 3$ and $2x + 3y < 12$.

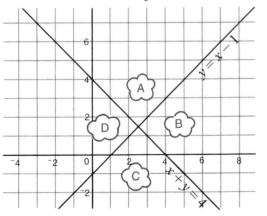

B6 The two lines $x + y = 4$ and $y = x - 1$ divide the plane into four regions A, B, C and D.

Write down the pair of inequalities which describes each of the four regions A, B, C and D.

B7 Draw the region described by the two inequalities $y > x^2$ and $y < 2x$.

B8 Draw the region described by the two inequalities $y > x(x - 2)$ and $y < x(4 - x)$.

c Graphing constraints

A dressmaker makes skirts and trousers from woollen material. Each skirt needs 2 metres of material and takes 1 hour to make. Each pair of trousers needs 2·5 metres of material and takes 2 hours to make.

The dressmaker has 15 metres of material available and a maximum of 10 hours in which to work. What combinations of skirts and trousers can she make?

This problem looks similar to some of those you met in the earlier chapter on optimisation. The difference here is that there is **more than one constraint**.

1st constraint   The amount of material must not exceed 15 metres.
2nd constraint   The time taken must not be more than 10 hours.

When there are two or more constraints, going through the possible combinations of garments in a systematic way can get rather complicated, because the effects of all the constraints have to be taken into account as you go.

However, if there are only two kinds of item to combine (as here, with skirts and trousers), there is a graphical method which can be used to represent the allowable combinations.

1 Suppose the dressmaker makes x skirts and y pairs of trousers.

2 Look at the first constraint – the amount of material available.

x skirts use up x times 2 metres, or $2x$ metres.
y pairs of trousers use up y times 2·5 metres, or $2 \cdot 5y$ metres.

The total amount must be less than or equal to 15 metres. So

$$2x + 2 \cdot 5y \leqslant 15.$$

$\leqslant$ means 'less than or equal to'.

3 x and y cannot be negative numbers, so we can forget about negative values of x and y.

Draw the line $2x + 2 \cdot 5y = 15$.

By using a test point we find that the region $2x + 2 \cdot 5y < 15$ is **below** the line.

The region $2x + 2 \cdot 5y \leqslant 15$ includes the line itself as well.

Shade out the region where $2x + 2 \cdot 5y$ is greater than 15.

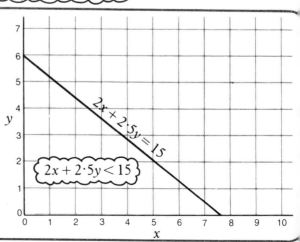

4 Now look at the second constraint – the time available

x skirts take x times 1 hour, or x hours.
y pairs of trousers take y times 2 hours, or $2y$ hours.

The total time available must be less than or equal to 10 hours. So

$x + 2y \leqslant 10$.

5 Draw the line whose equation is $x + 2y = 10$.

The region $x + 2y < 10$ is below the line.
The region $x + 2y \leqslant 10$ includes the line itself as well.

The points marked with dots show the only combinations which are allowed when **both** constraints have been taken into account.

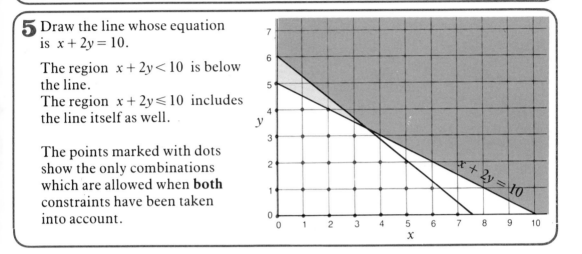

C1 Suppose the dressmaker makes a profit of £11 on each skirt, and a profit of £16 on each pair of trousers.

Which of the allowable combinations shown above will be the most profitable to make?

(For example, (4, 2) is an allowable combination. If she makes 4 skirts and 2 pairs of trousers her profit will be $4 \times £11 + 2 \times £16$. Can she do better than this?)

C2 A woman knits jumpers and cardigans from black and white wool. Each jumper needs 200 g of black wool and 100 g of white. Each cardigan needs 80 g of black and 250 g of white. The woman has 1000 g of each colour wool.

Suppose she makes x jumpers and y cardigans.
(a) Write down an inequality which says that the amount of black wool she uses is less than or equal to 1000 g.
(b) Draw axes with x and y from 0 to 15. Show the region described by the inequality.
(c) Write down an inequality which says that the amount of white wool used is less than or equal to 1000 g.
(d) Show on the graph the region described by this inequality.
(e) Mark a dot at each allowable combination of x and y.
(f) If the woman makes a profit of £10 on each jumper and £12 on each cardigan, find the most profitable combination.

C3   A children's outing is being planned. Two kinds of coach can be hired: small coaches carry 24 children and cost £50, and large coaches carry 40 children and cost £80.

At least 120 children want to go on the outing, but the cost of hiring the coaches must not be more than £400.

Let x be the number of small coaches hired and let y be the number of large coaches hired.

(a) Write down an expression for the number of children who can be carried altogether in x small coaches and y large coaches.

(b) Write down an inequality which says that the total number of children carried must be at least 120 (or, in other words, greater than or equal to 120).

(c) Draw axes with x and y from 0 to 8. Draw the region described by the inequality.

(d) Write down an expression for the total cost in £ of hiring x small coaches and y large coaches.

(e) Write down an inequality which says that the total cost must not be more than £400.

(f) On your diagram show the region described by this inequality and the previous one. Mark a dot at each allowable combination of x and y.

(g) Find out which combination is the cheapest.

(h) Find out which combination maximises the number of children who can be taken on the outing.

(i) For each of the allowable combinations, work out the cost per child, assuming that all coaches are filled. (To do this, you work out the total cost of a combination and divide it by the number of children who can be carried.)

Which combination gives the smallest cost per child?

C4   A train ferry can accommodate trains made up of coaches and goods vans, up to a maximum total length of 160 m and a maximum total weight of 480 tonnes.

Each coach is 20 m long and weighs 40 tonnes. Each goods van is 16 m long and weighs 60 tonnes.

Suppose a train consists of x coaches and y goods vans.

(a) Write down an inequality based on the maximum length of the train.

(b) Write down an inequality based on the maximum weight.

(c) Draw a graph to show the region which satisfies both inequalities.

(d) What is the maximum number of vehicles (coaches or goods vans) that the ferry can carry?

12 Vector geometry

A Displacement vectors

If a small object is moved from one place to another, we say it
undergoes a **displacement**.

The displacement can be represented by an arrow, called a
displacement vector, whose length and direction show the
length and direction of the displacement.

When a large object is **translated**, every point
of it moves the same distance and in the same
direction.

We say the displacements of the points are all
equal.

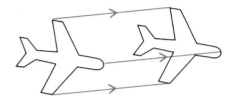

'Equal' here means 'having the same length and the same direction'.
So, for example, these two displacement vectors are equal:

But these are **not** equal:

(Same length, but different directions)

And neither are these:

(Same direction, but different lengths)

The vector which starts at a point A and ends at B
is written $\overrightarrow{AB}$. In the diagram on the right, the vector
$\overrightarrow{AB}$ is equal to the vector $\overrightarrow{CD}$, so we write $\overrightarrow{AB} = \overrightarrow{CD}$.

Often we use a single small letter with a squiggle to
stand for a vector. If $\overrightarrow{AB}$ is called $\underset{\sim}{u}$, then because
$\overrightarrow{CD}$ is equal to $\overrightarrow{AB}$, $\overrightarrow{CD} = \underset{\sim}{u}$ as well.

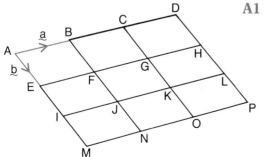

A1 This is a grid of congruent parallelograms.
The vector $\overrightarrow{AB}$ is called $\underset{\sim}{a}$.
The vector $\overrightarrow{AE}$ is called $\underset{\sim}{b}$.

(a) Write down as many vectors as you can
which are equal to $\underset{\sim}{a}$ (for example, $\overrightarrow{FG}$).

(b) Write down as many vectors as you can
which are equal to $\underset{\sim}{b}$.

135

In this diagram, the vector $\overrightarrow{AC}$ is twice as long as $\overrightarrow{AB}$ and in the same direction.

We write $\overrightarrow{AC} = 2\underset{\sim}{a}$.

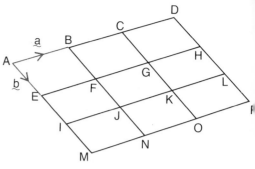

A2 (a) Write down two vectors each equal to $2\underset{\sim}{b}$.

(b) Write down two vectors each equal to $3\underset{\sim}{a}$.

The vector $\overrightarrow{FE}$ is the same length as $\overrightarrow{AB}$ but in the **opposite** direction.
We write $\overrightarrow{FE} = {}^{-}\underset{\sim}{a}$.

A3 (a) Write down two more vectors each equal to ${}^{-}\underset{\sim}{a}$.
(b) Write down two vectors each equal to ${}^{-}\underset{\sim}{b}$.

The vector $\overrightarrow{GE}$ is twice as long as $\overrightarrow{AB}$ but in the opposite direction.
We write $\overrightarrow{GE} = {}^{-}2\underset{\sim}{a}$.

A4 (a) Write down two more vectors each equal to ${}^{-}2\underset{\sim}{a}$.
(b) Write down two vectors each equal to ${}^{-}3\underset{\sim}{b}$.

B Adding and subtracting vectors

Let $\underset{\sim}{u}$ and $\underset{\sim}{v}$ be these two vectors:

We add two vectors by putting them 'end to end'. In other words, $\underset{\sim}{u} + \underset{\sim}{v}$ means 'do displacement $\underset{\sim}{u}$ first, then displacement $\underset{\sim}{v}$', as shown here:

The single displacement which takes us from the start of $\underset{\sim}{u}$ to the end of $\underset{\sim}{v}$ is called the vector sum of $\underset{\sim}{u}$ and $\underset{\sim}{v}$, and is written $\underset{\sim}{u} + \underset{\sim}{v}$.

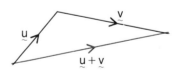

Notice that the length of $\underset{\sim}{u} + \underset{\sim}{v}$ is not the same as the length of $\underset{\sim}{u}$ + the length of $\underset{\sim}{v}$. Adding two vectors is a different kind of thing from adding two lengths.

Notice that if you change the order and do $\underset{\sim}{v} + \underset{\sim}{u}$, the results are equal.

So $\underset{\sim}{u} + \underset{\sim}{v} = \underset{\sim}{v} + \underset{\sim}{u}$ for any pair of vectors.

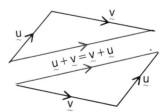

If you want to add together $2\underset{\sim}{u}$ and $3\underset{\sim}{v}$, you do it like this:

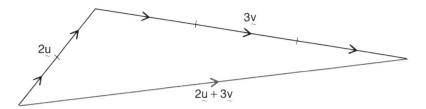

B1 Draw any two vectors (in different directions) and call them $\underset{\sim}{a}$ and $\underset{\sim}{b}$. Make them fairly short, for example

Draw a diagram for each of these.

(a) $\underset{\sim}{a} + \underset{\sim}{b}$ (b) $2\underset{\sim}{a} + \underset{\sim}{b}$ (c) $2\underset{\sim}{a} + 2\underset{\sim}{b}$

Let $\underset{\sim}{u}$ and $\underset{\sim}{v}$ be these two vectors:

Just as with numbers 'subtract 3' is the same as 'add $^-3$', so with vectors 'subtract $\underset{\sim}{v}$' is the same as 'add $^-\underset{\sim}{v}$'.

$^-\underset{\sim}{v}$ is the vector you get by reversing the direction of $\underset{\sim}{v}$:

So to find $\underset{\sim}{u} - \underset{\sim}{v}$, you do $\underset{\sim}{u} + {}^-\underset{\sim}{v}$.

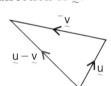

B2 Use the vectors $\underset{\sim}{a}$ and $\underset{\sim}{b}$ you drew for question B1. Draw a diagram for each of these.

(a) $\underset{\sim}{a} - \underset{\sim}{b}$ (b) $\underset{\sim}{b} - \underset{\sim}{a}$ (c) $2\underset{\sim}{a} - \underset{\sim}{b}$ (d) $\underset{\sim}{a} - 2\underset{\sim}{b}$

B3 ABCD is a rectangle whose diagonals cross at E.
$\overrightarrow{DE} = \underset{\sim}{u}$ and $\overrightarrow{EC} = \underset{\sim}{v}$.

(a) Write down a vector equal to $\underset{\sim}{u} + \underset{\sim}{v}$.

(b) Write down another vector equal to $\underset{\sim}{u} + \underset{\sim}{v}$.

(c) Write down two vectors each equal to $\underset{\sim}{u} - \underset{\sim}{v}$.

(d) Write down two vectors each equal to $\underset{\sim}{v} - \underset{\sim}{u}$.

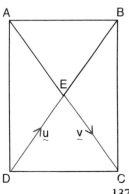

Expressing vectors in terms of given vectors

ABCD is a trapezium.
DC is parallel to AB and twice as long
as AB.

The vectors $\overrightarrow{AB}$ and $\overrightarrow{AD}$ have been called
u and v.

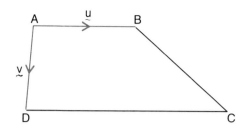

We shall show how all the other vectors in the diagram, including those
obtained by drawing the diagonals, can be expressed in terms of u and v.

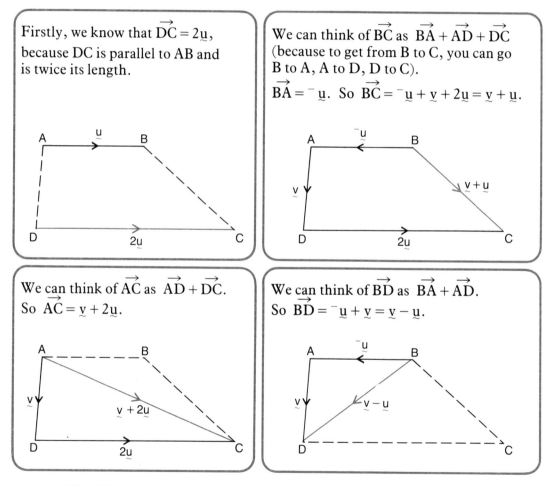

Firstly, we know that $\overrightarrow{DC} = 2u$,
because DC is parallel to AB and
is twice its length.

We can think of $\overrightarrow{BC}$ as $\overrightarrow{BA} + \overrightarrow{AD} + \overrightarrow{DC}$
(because to get from B to C, you can go
B to A, A to D, D to C).
$\overrightarrow{BA} = {}^-u$. So $\overrightarrow{BC} = {}^-u + v + 2u = v + u$.

We can think of $\overrightarrow{AC}$ as $\overrightarrow{AD} + \overrightarrow{DC}$.
So $\overrightarrow{AC} = v + 2u$.

We can think of $\overrightarrow{BD}$ as $\overrightarrow{BA} + \overrightarrow{AD}$.
So $\overrightarrow{BD} = {}^-u + v = v - u$.

C1 Write down an expression for each of these vectors in the
diagram above, in terms of u and v.

(a) $\overrightarrow{DA}$ (b) $\overrightarrow{DB}$ (c) $\overrightarrow{CD}$ (d) $\overrightarrow{CA}$ (e) $\overrightarrow{CB}$

C2 ABCD is a parallelogram.

$\overrightarrow{AB} = \underset{\sim}{a}$ and $\overrightarrow{AD} = \underset{\sim}{b}$.

Express in terms of $\underset{\sim}{a}$ and $\underset{\sim}{b}$

(a) $\overrightarrow{AC}$ (b) $\overrightarrow{BD}$ (c) $\overrightarrow{DB}$

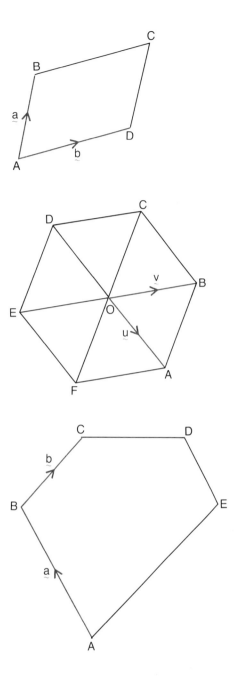

C3 ABCDEF is a regular hexagon. Its diagonals cross at O.

$\overrightarrow{OA} = \underset{\sim}{u}$ and $\overrightarrow{OB} = \underset{\sim}{v}$.

Express each of these vectors in terms of $\underset{\sim}{u}$ and $\underset{\sim}{v}$.

(a) $\overrightarrow{DA}$ (b) $\overrightarrow{BE}$ (c) $\overrightarrow{AB}$

(d) $\overrightarrow{FC}$ (e) $\overrightarrow{FB}$ (f) $\overrightarrow{FD}$

C4 In this diagram, AE is parallel to BC, and twice as long as BC.

ED is parallel to AB, and half as long as AB.

$\overrightarrow{AB} = \underset{\sim}{a}$ and $\overrightarrow{BC} = \underset{\sim}{b}$.

Express each of these in terms of $\underset{\sim}{a}$ and $\underset{\sim}{b}$.

(a) $\overrightarrow{AE}$ (b) $\overrightarrow{ED}$ (c) $\overrightarrow{AC}$

(d) $\overrightarrow{BE}$ (e) $\overrightarrow{AD}$ (f) $\overrightarrow{CD}$

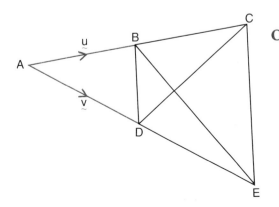

C5 In this diagram, the lengths AB and BC are equal, and the lengths AD and DE are equal.

$\overrightarrow{AB} = \underset{\sim}{u}$ and $\overrightarrow{AD} = \underset{\sim}{v}$.

Express these in terms of $\underset{\sim}{u}$ and $\underset{\sim}{v}$.

(a) $\overrightarrow{AC}$ (b) $\overrightarrow{AE}$ (c) $\overrightarrow{DC}$

(d) $\overrightarrow{BE}$ (e) $\overrightarrow{BD}$ (f) $\overrightarrow{CE}$

In question C5, parts (e) and (f), you should have found that

$$\overrightarrow{BD} = {}^-u + v + v - u,$$

$$\overrightarrow{CE} = {}^-2u + 2v = 2v - 2u.$$

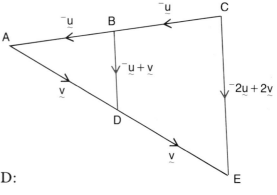

Notice that $2v - 2u$ can be written as $2(v - u)$.

So it follows that $\overrightarrow{CE} = 2\overrightarrow{BD}$.

This vector statement can be translated into a statement about the lines CE and BD:

> The line CE is parallel to the line BD and twice as long as BD.

This is an example of a geometrical fact which can be proved using vectors. In the next section we shall see how vectors can be used to prove some other facts.

D Proving by vectors

Worked example

In this diagram, $\overrightarrow{OA} = a$ and $\overrightarrow{OB} = b$.

$\overrightarrow{OC} = 2a$, $\overrightarrow{OD} = 3a$, $\overrightarrow{OE} = 3b$ and $\overrightarrow{OF} = 4b$.

G is the midpoint of CF.

(a) Express in terms of a and b

    (i) $\overrightarrow{CF}$ (ii) $\overrightarrow{CG}$ (iii) $\overrightarrow{DG}$ (iv) $\overrightarrow{DE}$

(b) What can you say about the points D, G and E?

(a) (i) $\overrightarrow{CF} = \overrightarrow{CO} + \overrightarrow{OF} = {}^-2a + 4b.$

    (ii) $\overrightarrow{CG} = \tfrac{1}{2}\overrightarrow{CF} = \tfrac{1}{2}({}^-2a + 4b) = {}^-a + 2b.$

    (iii) $\overrightarrow{DG} = \overrightarrow{DC} + \overrightarrow{CG} = {}^-a + ({}^-a + 2b) = {}^-2a + 2b.$

    (iv) $\overrightarrow{DE} = \overrightarrow{DO} + \overrightarrow{OE} = {}^-3a + 3b.$

(b) Look at the expressions for $\overrightarrow{DG}$ and $\overrightarrow{DE}$: $\overrightarrow{DG} = {}^-2a + 2b = 2({}^-a + b),$

$$\overrightarrow{DE} = {}^-3a + 3b = 3({}^-a + b).$$

So $\overrightarrow{DE} = 1\tfrac{1}{2}\overrightarrow{DG}$. It follows that **D, G and E must be in a straight line.**

In the worked example we **proved** that D, G and E are in a straight line. We did this by finding expressions for $\vec{DG}$ and $\vec{DE}$, and then showing that $\vec{DE}$ can be written as 'a number $\times \vec{DG}$' (in this case $\vec{DE} = 1\frac{1}{2}\vec{DG}$).

The next questions are similar examples of this method of proving that three points are in a straight line.

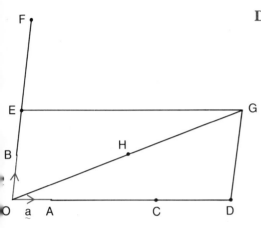

D1 In this diagram, $\vec{OA} = \underset{\sim}{a}$ and $\vec{OB} = \underset{\sim}{b}$.

$\vec{OC} = 4\underset{\sim}{a}$, $\vec{OD} = 6\underset{\sim}{a}$, $\vec{OE} = 2\underset{\sim}{b}$, $\vec{OF} = 4\underset{\sim}{b}$.

ODGE is a parallelogram.
H is the midpoint of OG.

(a) Express in terms of $\underset{\sim}{a}$ and $\underset{\sim}{b}$

    (i) $\vec{OG}$ (ii) $\vec{OH}$

(b) Use the fact that $\vec{CF} = \vec{CO} + \vec{OF}$ to write an expression for $\vec{CF}$ in terms of $\underset{\sim}{a}$ and $\underset{\sim}{b}$.

(c) Use the fact that $\vec{CH} = \vec{CO} + \vec{OH}$ to write an expression for $\vec{CH}$ in terms of $\underset{\sim}{a}$ and $\underset{\sim}{b}$.

(d) What is the relation between the vectors $\vec{CF}$ and $\vec{CH}$?

(e) What can you deduce about the points C, H and F?

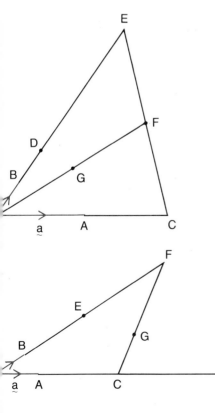

D2 In this diagram, $\vec{OA} = \underset{\sim}{a}$ and $\vec{OB} = \underset{\sim}{b}$.

$\vec{OC} = 2\underset{\sim}{a}$, $\vec{OD} = 2\underset{\sim}{b}$, $\vec{OE} = 6\underset{\sim}{b}$.

F is the midpoint of CE, and G is the midpoint of OF.

(a) Use the fact that $\vec{DC} = \vec{DO} + \vec{OC}$ to express $\vec{DC}$ in terms of $\underset{\sim}{a}$ and $\underset{\sim}{b}$.

(b) Express in terms of $\underset{\sim}{a}$ and $\underset{\sim}{b}$ (i) $\vec{CE}$

   (ii) $\vec{CF}$ (iii) $\vec{OF}$ (iv) $\vec{OG}$ (v) $\vec{DG}$

(c) Use your answers to (a) and (b) part (v) to state the relation between $\vec{DC}$ and $\vec{DG}$.

(d) Deduce a fact about the points D, G and C.

D3 In this diagram, $\vec{OC} = 3\underset{\sim}{a}$, $\vec{OD} = 6\underset{\sim}{a}$,
$\vec{OE} = 3\underset{\sim}{b}$ and $\vec{OF} = 6\underset{\sim}{b}$.
G is one-third of the way along CF.

(a) Express in terms of $\underset{\sim}{a}$ and $\underset{\sim}{b}$ the vectors $\vec{CF}$, $\vec{CG}$, $\vec{EG}$ and $\vec{ED}$.

(b) State the relation between $\vec{ED}$ and $\vec{EG}$.

141

Position vectors

Suppose we choose a point in a plane and call it O.

If A is any other point in the plane, the vector $\overrightarrow{OA}$ is called the **position vector** of A relative to O.

If we agree that all position vectors will start out from the same point O, then we do not need to say 'relative to O'. We just say that $\overrightarrow{OA}$ is the position vector of A, $\overrightarrow{OB}$ is the position vector of B, and so on.

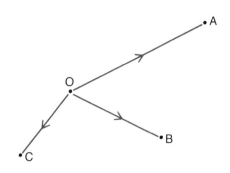

E1 This is part of a grid of congruent parallelograms.
The position vector of A is $\underset{\sim}{a}$.
The position vector of B is $\underset{\sim}{b}$.

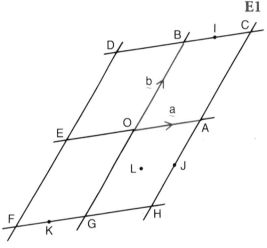

Write down in terms of $\underset{\sim}{a}$ and $\underset{\sim}{b}$ the position vector of each of these points.

(a) C (b) D (c) E (d) F (e) G (f) H

(g) I (the midpoint of BC)

(h) J (the midpoint of AH)

(i) K (the midpoint of FG)

(j) L (the centre of parallelogram OAHG)

E2 ABCDEF is a regular hexagon.
O is at the centre of the hexagon.

The position vector of A is $\underset{\sim}{a}$.
The position vector of C is $\underset{\sim}{c}$.

Write down in terms of $\underset{\sim}{a}$ and $\underset{\sim}{c}$ the position vector of each of the other vertices of the hexagon.

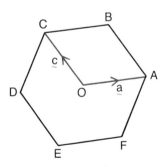

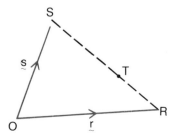

E3 In the diagram on the left, $\overrightarrow{OR} = \underset{\sim}{r}$ and $\overrightarrow{OS} = \underset{\sim}{s}$.

(a) Express the vector $\overrightarrow{RS}$ in terms of $\underset{\sim}{r}$ and $\underset{\sim}{s}$.

(b) T is one-third of the way along RS.
Express $\overrightarrow{RT}$ in terms of $\underset{\sim}{r}$ and $\underset{\sim}{s}$.

(c) Write down the position vector of T ($\overrightarrow{OT}$) in terms of $\underset{\sim}{r}$ and $\underset{\sim}{s}$.

E4 In the diagram on the right,
OA = a and OB = b.

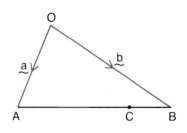

The point C is $\frac{3}{4}$ of the way along AB.

(a) Express $\overrightarrow{AB}$ in terms of a and b.

(b) Express $\overrightarrow{AC}$ in terms of a and b.

(c) Write down the position vector of C, in terms of a and b.

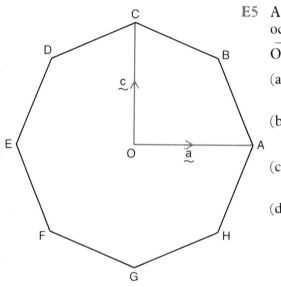

E5 A, B and C are three vertices of a regular octagon, whose centre is at O.

$\overrightarrow{OA} = a$ and $\overrightarrow{OC} = c$.

(a) Draw the diagram and mark the point X whose position vector is a + c.

(b) If $\overrightarrow{OA}$ and $\overrightarrow{OC}$ are each 1 unit long, what is the length of $\overrightarrow{OX}$?

(c) Show that the position vector of B is approximately $0·707\,(a + c)$.

(d) Write down the position vector of all the other vertices of the octagon, in terms of a and c.

E6 O is the centre of the regular hexagon ABCDEF.

$\overrightarrow{OA}$ = a and $\overrightarrow{OB}$ = b.

Find, in terms of a and b, the position vector of

(a) the midpoint of AB

(b) the midpoint of BC

(c) the midpoint of CD

(d) the midpoint of DE

(e) the midpoint of EF

(f) the midpoint of FA

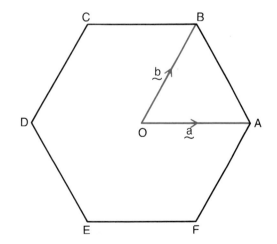

9 Iteration

9.1 The iteration formula of a sequence s is $s_{n+1} = \dfrac{s_n + 1}{5}$.

(a) Start with $s_1 = 0$ and calculate $s_2, s_3, \ldots$ up to s_8.

(b) What limit do you think the sequence converges towards?

(c) Check that this limit is a fixed point of the iteration formula.

9.2 By solving an equation, calculate the fixed point(s) of each of these iteration formulas.

(a) $t_{n+1} = \dfrac{2t_n + 7}{4}$ (b) $t_{n+1} = \dfrac{4}{t_n + 3}$

9.3 The iteration formula for a sequence u is $u_{n+1} = \sqrt{(u_n + 1)}$

(a) Start with $u_1 = 0$ and calculate $u_2, u_3, \ldots$ until the second decimal place no longer changes.

(b) Write down the limit of the sequence to 2 decimal places.

9.4 (a) Make a table of values of the function $x \to x(x-3)$ for values of x from $^-2$ to 5.

(b) Draw a graph of the function.

(c) From the graph estimate, to 1 decimal place, the values of x for which $x(x-3) = 1$.

(d) Use iteration formulas to find the values of both solutions of the equation $x(x-3) = 1$, correct to 2 d.p.

10 The sine and cosine functions (2)

10.1 The graph on the right is the graph of one of these functions. Which one is it?

$\theta \to \sin 2\theta$ $\theta \to \sin \tfrac{1}{2}\theta$

$\theta \to 2\sin\theta$ $\theta \to \tfrac{1}{2}\sin\theta$

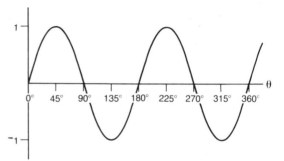

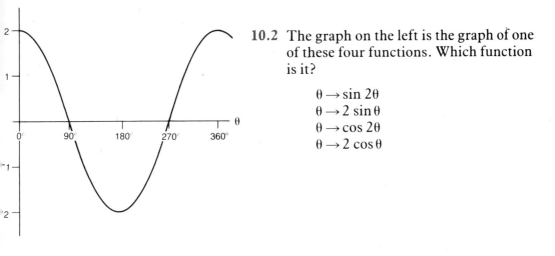

10.2 The graph on the left is the graph of one of these four functions. Which function is it?

$$\theta \to \sin 2\theta$$
$$\theta \to 2 \sin \theta$$
$$\theta \to \cos 2\theta$$
$$\theta \to 2 \cos \theta$$

11 Inequalities

11.1 Draw axes with values of x and y from $^-5$ to 5.
Draw the line whose equation is $2x - 3y = 6$.
Show the region $2x - 3y > 6$ by shading out the unwanted part.

11.2 Write down inequalities which describe the unshaded regions below.

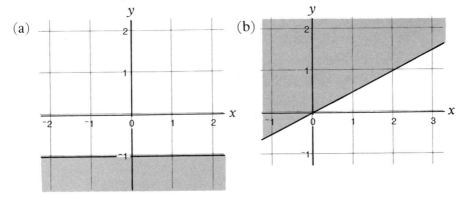

(a)   (b)

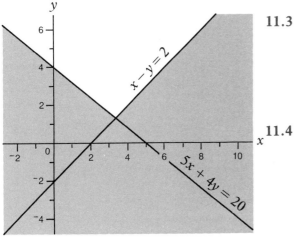

11.3 Write down a pair of inequalities which describes the unshaded region here.

(You may find it useful to choose a 'test point' somewhere in the region.)

11.4 Draw axes with x and y from $^-3$ to 3. Indicate clearly the region described by the two inequalities $y > x$ and $y < 2 - x^2$.

145

11.5 A factory employs unskilled workers who earn £120 a week and skilled workers who earn £240 a week.
The weekly wage bill must not exceed £21 600.

The machines need a minimum of 105 operators, of whom at least 40 must be skilled.

Union regulations require that the number of skilled workers should be at least half the number of unskilled workers.

(a) Show that $x + 2y \leqslant 180$.

(b) Write down three other inequalities which x and y have to satisfy (other than $x \geqslant 0, y \geqslant 0$).

(c) Represent all four inequalities on a graph, shading out the unwanted region.

(d) Use your graph to find the range within which the number of unskilled workers must lie.

12 Vector geometry

12.1 In this diagram, DC is parallel to AB and twice the length of AB.

$\overrightarrow{AB} = \underset{\sim}{r}$ and $\overrightarrow{AC} = \underset{\sim}{s}$.

Express each of these vectors in terms of $\underset{\sim}{r}$ and $\underset{\sim}{s}$.

(a) $\overrightarrow{AC}$ (b) $\overrightarrow{DC}$ (c) $\overrightarrow{AD}$ (d) $\overrightarrow{BD}$

12.2 OACB is a parallelogram.
D is the midpoint of AC.
E is the midpoint of BC.

$\overrightarrow{OA} = \underset{\sim}{a}$ and $\overrightarrow{OB} = \underset{\sim}{b}$.

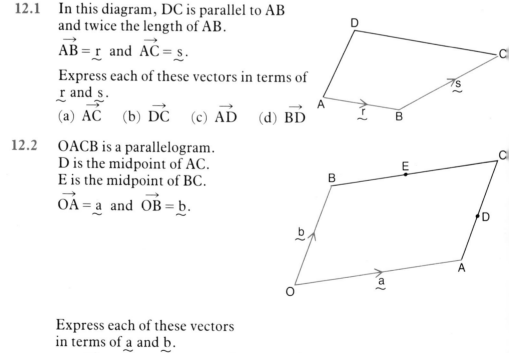

Express each of these vectors in terms of $\underset{\sim}{a}$ and $\underset{\sim}{b}$.

(a) $\overrightarrow{OC}$ (b) $\overrightarrow{OD}$ (c) $\overrightarrow{OE}$ (d) $\overrightarrow{CE}$

(e) $\overrightarrow{AE}$ (f) $\overrightarrow{DB}$ (g) $\overrightarrow{ED}$ (h) $\overrightarrow{EO}$

12.3 X is the midpoint of AB.
Y is the midpoint of AC.
$\overrightarrow{XB} = \underset{\sim}{u}$ and $\overrightarrow{XC} = \underset{\sim}{v}$.

Express each of these vectors
in terms of $\underset{\sim}{u}$ and $\underset{\sim}{v}$.

(a) $\overrightarrow{AB}$ (b) $\overrightarrow{BC}$ (c) $\overrightarrow{AC}$

(d) $\overrightarrow{AY}$ (e) $\overrightarrow{BY}$ (f) $\overrightarrow{XY}$

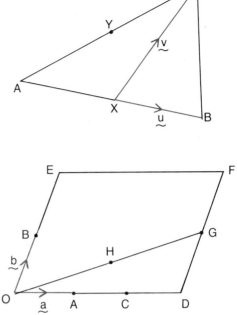

12.4 ODFE is a parallelogram.
$\overrightarrow{OA} = \underset{\sim}{a}$, $\overrightarrow{OC} = 2\underset{\sim}{a}$, $\overrightarrow{OD} = 3\underset{\sim}{a}$.
$\overrightarrow{OB} = \underset{\sim}{b}$, $\overrightarrow{OE} = 2\underset{\sim}{b}$.

G is the midpoint of DF.
H is the midpoint of OG.

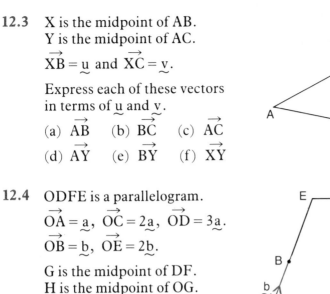

(a) Express $\overrightarrow{CE}$ in terms of $\underset{\sim}{a}$ and $\underset{\sim}{b}$.

(b) Express each of these vectors in terms of $\underset{\sim}{a}$ and $\underset{\sim}{b}$.

   (i) $\overrightarrow{OG}$ (ii) $\overrightarrow{OH}$ (iii) $\overrightarrow{CH}$

(c) Show that $\overrightarrow{CE} = 4\overrightarrow{CH}$, and deduce a fact about the
points C, H and E.

12.5 OABCDE is a regular hexagon.
$\overrightarrow{OA} = \underset{\sim}{a}$ and $\overrightarrow{OE} = \underset{\sim}{e}$.

Find in terms of $\underset{\sim}{a}$ and $\underset{\sim}{b}$.

(a) the position vector of B
   (i.e. the vector $\overrightarrow{OB}$)

(b) the position vector of C

(c) the position vector of D

(d) the position vector of the
   midpoint of AB

(e) the position vector of the
   midpoint of BC

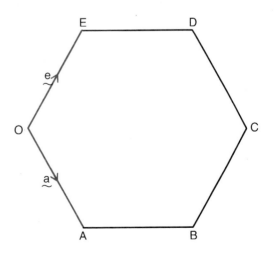

Whole numbers and decimals

1.1 Without using a calculator, say which of these you could buy with a £20 note.
(a) 38 metres of hosepipe at 47p per metre
(b) 4·5 metres of curtain fabric at £5·25 per metre
(c) 120 metres of nylon rope at 21p per metre

1.2 When Brenda puts her gas fire on 'high', the gas it uses costs 68p per hour. How much does it cost to have it on
(a) for 8 hours   (b) for $2\frac{1}{4}$ hours
(c) over the weekend, from 6 p.m. Friday to 8 a.m. Monday

1.3 (a) 6 people share a 5 kg sack of potatoes. What weight does each get?
(b) 5 people share a 6 kg sack. What weight does each get?

1.4 A station buffet sells coffee in standard cups (240 ml) at 38p, or in large beakers (330 ml) at 55p. Which is better value?

1.5 This picture shows a sheet of stick-on labels. Each label is 2·5 cm wide and 1·5 cm high. The sheet is 65 cm wide and 48 cm high.

How many labels are there on the sheet?

1.6 A bottle contains 0·6 litre of cough mixture. The 'adult dose' is three medicine spoonfuls. A medicine spoon holds 5 ml.

How many adult doses can you get from the bottle?

1.7 Round off   (a) 37·886 to 2 d.p.   (b) 37·886 to 2 s.f.
(c) 0·039 862 to 3 s.f.   (d) 362 598 to 3 s.f.

1.8 Write these numbers in standard index form.
(a) 20 000 000   (b) 0·000 08   (c) 3 620 000   (d) 0·000 009 27

1.9 The value of a is known to be somewhere between 2·4 and 2·5. The value of b is known to be somewhere between 4·8 and 5·0.

(a) Calculate the minimum and maximum possible values of ab.
(b) Calculate the minimum and maximum possible values of $\frac{a}{b}$.

1.10 A racing car was timed over a measured distance. The distance was 500·0 metres, correct to the nearest 0·1 m. The time taken was 4·58 seconds, correct to the nearest 0·01 second.

    (a) State the minimum and maximum possible values for the actual distance travelled by the car.

    (b) Do the same for the actual time taken.

    (c) Calculate, to 2 d.p., maximum and minimum values for the average speed of the car, in m/s.

2 Percentage

2.1 Calculate   (a) 45% of £280   (b) 8% of £17·50

	Male	Female
Under 18	23	19
18 or over	63	70

2.2 This table gives some information about 175 people living in a block of flats.

    (a) What percentage of the 175 people are males aged 18 or over?

    (b) What percentage are females under 18?

    (c) What percentage **of the males** are under 18?

    (d) What percentage of the under-18s are male?

2.3 (a) Alice's salary is £8260. It goes up by 15%. What is it after the increase?

    (b) Ada's salary goes up from £7230 to £8240. What is the percentage increase?

2.4 Calculate the percentage reduction in each of these, to the nearest 1%.

    (a) A car salesman reduces the price of a car from £3000 to £2750.

    (b) An estate agent reduces the price of a house from £49 500 to £47 500.

    (c) A dress shop reduces the price of a £75 dress by £20.

2.5 (a) Between January 1986 and January 1987, the average price of a house on Meadowside went up by 7%. What is the multiplier from the January 1986 price to the January 1987 price?

Jan 1986 price ——| ×? ⟩→ Jan 1987 price

    (b) Between January 1987 and January 1988, the average price went up by 12%. Calculate the overall percentage increase between January 1986 and January 1988.

2.6 In March a camera shop raised the price of a camera by 16%. In September they had a sale, in which all prices were reduced by 15%.

Was the sale price higher or lower than the price before March? Give the reason for your answer.

2.7 A newspaper reporting a flu epidemic in a village said that women had been worse affected than men. It stated that out of 450 cases of flu, 271 were women and 179 men.

	Caught flu	Did not catch flu
Men	179	88
Women	271	159

The actual data on which the paper based its conclusion is shown in this table. Do you agree with the paper's conclusion? If not, state your reasons clearly.

3 Fractions

3.1 The sizes of five nuts (in inches) are $\frac{11''}{16}$, $\frac{1''}{2}$, $\frac{5''}{8}$, $\frac{15''}{16}$ and $\frac{3''}{4}$. Put them in order of size, starting with the smallest.

3.2 You are trying to tighten a bolt. A $\frac{3''}{4}$ spanner is just too small. A $\frac{7''}{8}$ spanner is just too big. Which size is halfway between the two?

3.3 1 inch is equal to 25·4 mm.
What are these equal to in mm, to the nearest 0·1 mm?

(a) $\frac{1''}{4}$ (b) $\frac{3''}{4}$ (c) $\frac{5''}{8}$ (d) $\frac{13''}{16}$

3.4 On a rabbit farm, $\frac{2}{5}$ of the rabbits are male, and $\frac{3}{4}$ of the male rabbits are white. What fraction of all the rabbits are white males?

4 Ratio

4.1 The 'aspect ratio' of a cinema screen is the ratio $\frac{\text{width}}{\text{height}}$.

(a) Calculate the aspect ratio of each of these screens, to 2 d.p.

A: 5·7 m wide, 4·3 m high   B: 10·6 m wide, 5·2 m high
C: 7·8 m wide, 5·2 m high   D: 7·2 m wide, 4·8 m high

(b) Which of the four screens are similar to each other?

4.2 Calculate these multipliers, to 3 significant figures.

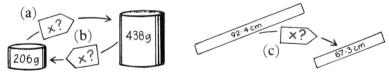

4.3 In an equilateral triangle, the ratio $\frac{\text{height}}{\text{base}}$ is 0·866 (to 3 s.f.).

Use this fact to calculate
(a) the height of an equilateral triangle whose base is 4·5 cm
(b) the base of an equilateral triangle whose height is 7·2 cm

4.4 A grocer mixes good quality and poor quality tea in the ratio 3 to 5 by weight. What percentage of the mixture is good quality tea?

5 Gradient

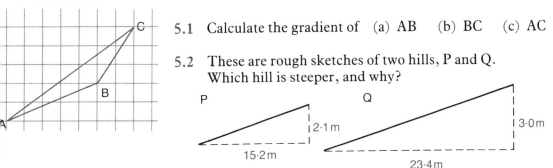

5.1 Calculate the gradient of (a) AB   (b) BC   (c) AC

5.2 These are rough sketches of two hills, P and Q.
Which hill is steeper, and why?

P   Q

2·1 m   3·0 m

15·2 m   23·4 m

5.3 Calculate the gradient of the line joining
(a) $(0, 0)$ and $(4, {}^-2)$ (b) $({}^-1, 4)$ and $(4, 5)$ (c) $({}^-2, 5)$ and $(6, {}^-1)$

6 Rates

6.1 (a) A tap takes 12·5 minutes to fill a 60-litre water tank.
Calculate the rate of flow of the tap in litre/min.
(b) How long would it take to fill the same tank from a tap
which flows at 18·5 litre/min?

6.2 An oven is turned on. The temperature rises slowly at first, then
faster, and then more slowly again until it reaches a maximum.
Then it stays constant. Sketch a graph to show all this.

6.3 Worldwings Airways use AX7 aircraft on their flights from London
to Moscow, a distance of 1880 miles. The flight takes $4\frac{1}{4}$ hours.
(a) Calculate the average speed of the aircraft.
(b) The airline considers replacing the AX7 by another plane,
which can fly at an average speed of 530 m.p.h. If they
do this, what will the new flight time be?

6.4 This table shows distances and times for a train journey.

Distance from London (miles):	0		209	299		401
	London		Preston	Carlisle		Glasgow
Time:	12:45		15:30	16:45		18:15

(a) Calculate the average speed of the train between
(i) London and Preston   (ii) Preston and Carlisle
(iii) Carlisle and Glasgow
(b) Calculate the overall average speed for the whole journey, to 1 d.p.

6.5 A solution of copper sulphate contains 0·85 g of copper sulphate per litre.
(a) How much copper sulphate is there in 0·35 litre of solution?
(b) What volume of the solution contains 0·50 g of copper sulphate?

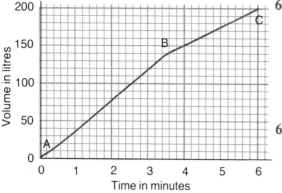

Volume in litres (y-axis: 0, 50, 100, 150, 200)
Time in minutes (x-axis: 0, 1, 2, 3, 4, 5, 6)

6.6 This graph shows the amount of liquid in a tank while it was being filled.

Calculate the average rate at which the water entered the tank
(a) between A and B
(b) between B and C

6.7 Pat is crossing the desert in a truck. She starts with a full fuel tank holding 140 litres of fuel. After travelling 80 m she has used up 25 litres.

She still has 390 miles to go. Will she make it?

7 Constructing formulas

7.1 These arrangements are made with red and black balls joined together.

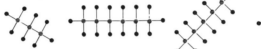

(a) How many black balls will there be when there are 20 red balls?

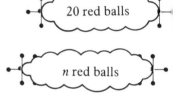
20 red balls

n red balls

(b) If there are n red balls in the arrangement, write down an expression for the number of black balls.

(c) If there are p black balls in an arrangement of this kind, write down an expression for the number of red balls.

7.2 (a) A box which weighs b kg empty contains n tins of paint, each weighing w kg. Write an expression for the total weight of the box and the tins of paint.

(b) A box of tennis balls weighs f kg when full of tennis balls and e kg when empty. There are n tennis balls in the box. Write an expression for the weight of one tennis ball.

7.3 A man leaves £a in his will, to be shared equally between his n children. Each child has to pay £1 in gift tax. Write an expression for the amount each child has after paying the tax.

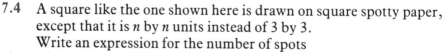

7.4 A square like the one shown here is drawn on square spotty paper, except that it is n by n units instead of 3 by 3. Write an expression for the number of spots
(a) on its boundary (b) inside the square

7.5 A small tin of milk weighs 170 g and costs 25p. A large tin weighs 410 g and costs 54p. I buy a small tins and b large tins.

Write down an expression for
(a) the total weight in grams   (b) the total cost in pence
(c) the amount of change I would get from £5

7.6 Water flows from a tap at a constant rate. x litres of water come out in y minutes. Write an expression for

(a) the rate of flow in litres per minute
(b) the rate of flow in litres per second
(c) the number of litres which come out in 1 hour

8 Techniques of algebra

8.1 If $a = 5$, $b = 2$ and $c = {}^-3$, calculate

(a) $a^2 + bc$ (b) $a - bc$ (c) $5b^2$ (d) $a(b - c)$ (e) $b^2 - 3c$
(f) $\dfrac{b - c}{a}$ (g) $\left(\dfrac{a - c}{b}\right)^2$ (h) $ab - c^2$ (i) $\dfrac{a}{b} + c$ (j) $\dfrac{a}{b + c}$

8.2 Calculate the value of $(3r - 4s)^2$ when
(a) $r = 5$, $s = 2$ (b) $r = 0{\cdot}5$, $s = 0{\cdot}6$ (c) $r = 1{\cdot}5$, $s = {}^-0{\cdot}5$

8.3 A printer was asked to print some equations. He was not able to print brackets so he just left them out. In each equation, p is 2, q is 3 and r is 7. Re-write them with brackets where necessary.

(a) $pqr + p = 46$ (b) $pq + qr = 48$ (c) $p + qp^2 = 64$
(d) $q + qr^2 = 150$ (e) $2q^2 + r = 43$ (f) $pr + qp^2 = 68$

8.4 If $k = 0{\cdot}6$, $l = 2{\cdot}3$, $m = 1{\cdot}9$ and $n = 5{\cdot}5$, calculate to 1 d.p.

(a) kl^2 (b) $\dfrac{km}{ln}$ (c) $2m^2 - 3k^2$ (d) $\dfrac{l}{m} + \dfrac{n}{k}$ (e) $\dfrac{n^2}{kml}$

8.5 If $p = 3{\cdot}6 \times 10^5$, $q = 1{\cdot}3 \times 10^{-4}$ and $r = 7{\cdot}0 \times 10^{-8}$, calculate the value of each of these, to 2 significant figures.

(a) pq (b) qr (c) q^2 (d) $\dfrac{p}{q}$ (e) $\dfrac{pr}{q}$ (f) $\dfrac{q}{pr}$

8.6 Multiply out the brackets in each of these expressions.
(a) $3(p + q)$ (b) $3(p + 2q)$ (c) $5(a - 3)$ (d) $a(b - a)$ (e) $xy(x + y)$

8.7 Simplify each of these expressions, where possible.
(a) $3n + 5 - 2n + 2$ (b) $5x - 3y - 12x - 4y$ (c) $a + 4 - 9 - 3a$
(d) $2b - 3c - 5 + a$ (e) $7u - 8 + 1 - 5u$ (f) $10 - 2x - 5 + 6x$
(g) $ab - 2a + a^2 + b^2$ (h) $3ab + 2a^2 + 5ab - a^2$

8.8 Remove the brackets from these expressions. Simplify if possible.
    (a) $3x + (5 - x)$ (b) $4x + 6 - (2 + 3x)$ (c) $10 - (2x - 3)$
    (d) $3x + 2(4 + x)$ (e) $6x - 3(x + 2)$ (f) $20 + 5(a - 4)$
    (g) $11 - 3(2 - 4x)$ (h) $p^2 - p(q - p)$ (i) $5(2x - 3) - 2(3x - 1)$

8.9 Factorise each of these expressions.
    (a) $3a + 6b$ (b) $4a - 12$ (c) $ab^2 + 5b$ (d) $8ab - 2a^2$ (e) $p^2q - pq^2$

8.10 Multiply out the brackets in each of these expressions.
    (a) $(x + 3)(y + 5)$ (b) $(x + 5)(2x + 1)$ (c) $(3x + 2)(2x - 5)$
    (d) $(3x - 4)^2$ (e) $(5x + 2)(5x - 2)$ (f) $(4 - 5x)^2$

8.11 Factorise each of these expressions.
    (a) $x^2 + 7x + 12$ (b) $x^2 - 2x - 15$ (c) $x^2 + x - 20$ (d) $x^2 - 6x + 8$

8.12 Write each of these as a single algebraic fraction.

    (a) $\dfrac{a}{b} \times \dfrac{c}{d}$ (b) $\dfrac{4}{x} \times \dfrac{x}{y}$ (c) $\left(\dfrac{x+y}{3}\right) \times \dfrac{2}{x}$ (d) $\dfrac{a}{2} \div \dfrac{b}{3}$ (e) $\dfrac{\left(\dfrac{a}{3x}\right)}{\left(\dfrac{b}{12x}\right)}$

8.13 Write each of these as a single algebraic fraction.
    (a) $\dfrac{5}{a} + \dfrac{2}{b}$ (b) $\dfrac{r}{s} - \dfrac{2r}{st}$ (c) $\dfrac{x}{3a} - \dfrac{y}{a^2}$ (d) $\dfrac{5}{x - 2} + \dfrac{3}{x}$ (e) $5x - \dfrac{3}{x}$

9 Solving equations and manipulating formulas

9.1 Solve each of these equations.
    (a) $3x - 17 = 28$ (b) $51 = 23 + 4x$ (c) $5x + 25 = 5$
    (d) $8x + 13 = 5x + 4$ (e) $6 - 3x = 2x - 4$ (f) $7 - x = 19 - 5x$

9.2 Solve each of these equations.
    (a) $\dfrac{3x - 2}{4} = 7$ (b) $2(3x - 1) = 16$ (c) $x = \dfrac{6 - x}{3}$

9.3 Solve these equations. Give the value of x to 2 d.p.
    (a) $2 \cdot 9x = 11 \cdot 3$ (b) $0 \cdot 83x = 0 \cdot 36$ (c) $\dfrac{x}{1 \cdot 6} = 0 \cdot 28$ (d) $\dfrac{3 \cdot 5}{x} = 0 \cdot 56$

9.4 P, V, R and T are connected by the equation $PV = RT$.
    (a) Write a formula for P in terms of the other letters.
    (b) Write a formula for V in terms of the other letters.
    (c) Write a formula for R in terms of the other letters.

9.5 u, v and m are connected by the formula $m = \dfrac{u}{v}$.

    (a) Re-arrange the formula to make u the subject.
    (b) Re-arrange the formula to make v the subject.

9.6 a, b, c and d are connected by the formula $d = ab + c$.
   (a) Calculate b, when $d = 37$, $a = 5$ and $c = 2$.
   (b) Calculate a, when $d = 13$, $b = 4$ and $c = 3$.
   (c) Re-arrange the formula so that c is the subject.
   (d) Re-arrange the formula so that a is the subject.

9.7 p, q, r and s related by the formula $r = \dfrac{p}{q} - s$.

   (a) Calculate p, when $r = 40$, $q = 3$ and $s = 2$.
   (b) Calculate s, when $r = 29$, $p = 10$ and $q = 2$.
   (c) Make p the subject of the formula.
   (d) Make s the subject of the formula.

9.8 Albert is 5 times as old as Gladys now. In 6 years' time, Albert will be only twice as old as Gladys.
Let x stand for Gladys's age now.

   (a) Write an expression for Albert's age now, in terms of x.
   (b) Write expressions for Gladys's age and for Albert's age in 6 years' time.
   (c) Write an equation which says that in 6 years' time, Albert will be twice as old as Gladys. Solve the equation to find Gladys's age now.

9.9 Anne has six times as much money as Mark. If she gives Mark £10 then she will have twice as much as Mark.
Solve an equation to find how much Mark has now.

9.10 Solve these equations. Give the value of x to 1 d.p.
   (a) $3 \cdot 2x - 0 \cdot 8 = 5 \cdot 1$ (b) $6 \cdot 7 - 1 \cdot 8x = 8 \cdot 5$ (c) $6 \cdot 1 = 8 \cdot 5 - 0 \cdot 3x$

9.11 Solve these equations.
   (a) $(x + 3)(x + 2) = x^2 + 24$ (b) $x(x - 3) = (x + 3)^2$

9.12 Make the letter printed in red the subject of each formula.
   (a) $s = \dfrac{ap}{qr}$ (b) $d = e - sf$ (c) $A = \dfrac{h(a + b)}{2}$ (d) $b = a(1 + rt)$

   (e) $a = \dfrac{v^2}{r}$ (f) $t = \sqrt{(au)}$ (g) $m = \dfrac{\sqrt{n}}{a}$ (h) $y = \sqrt{\left(\dfrac{a}{x}\right)}$

9.13 If $P = IV$ and $I = \dfrac{V}{R}$, find a formula for

   (a) P in terms of V and R (b) I in terms of P and V

   (c) V in terms of P and R (d) R in terms of P and V

9.14 If $x = 6y - z$ and $y = a + b$ and $z = 6 - b$, find a formula for x in terms of a and b, without brackets.

9.15 If $C = 2\pi r$ and $A = \pi r^2$, find a formula for A in terms of π and C.

9.16 Factorise the expression $x^2 + 5x + 6$, and use the result to solve the equation $x^2 + 5x + 6 = 0$.

9.17 Solve these equations by factorising.

(a) $x^2 - 2x - 8 = 0$ (b) $x^2 + x - 30 = 0$ (c) $x^2 - 5x = 0$

(d) $x^2 + 3x - 4 = 0$ (e) $x^2 - 8x + 15 = 0$ (f) $20 - 8x - x^2 = 0$

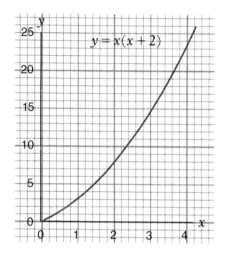

$y = x(x + 2)$

9.18 This is the graph of $y = x(x + 2)$ for values of x from 0 to 4.

(a) From the graph find, approximately, the value of x between 0 and 4 for which $x(x + 2) = 10$.

(b) Use the decimal search method to find this value, correct to 2 decimal places.

9.19 (a) Show that $x = 2 \cdot 6$ is an approximate solution of the equation $x^2 - x - 4 = 0$.

(b) Use the decimal search method to find this solution, correct to 2 d.p.

10 Linear equations and inequalities

10.1 Draw axes with x and y from $^-10$ to 10.

(a) Draw and label the line whose equation is $3x - 4y = 12$.

(b) The point $(1, 2)$ is above the line. Work out the value of $3x - 4y$ at $(1, 2)$.

(c) The point $(7, 0)$ is below the line. Work out the value of $3x - 4y$ at $(7, 0)$.

(d) Label clearly the region A where $3x - 4y < 12$, and the region B where $3x - 4y > 12$.

(e) Does the point $(6 \cdot 5, 1 \cdot 9)$ belong to region A or to region B?

10.2 The Hurts car-hire firm charges £10 per day plus 3p $(= £0 \cdot 03)$ per mile.

(a) If a car is hired for x days and driven for y miles, write down an expression for the hire charge, in £.

(b) The South Midland Parts Company's salespeople need to hire cars occasionally, but the company places a £90 upper limit on the cost of hire. Write down an inequality which expresses this fact.

(c) Draw axes with x from 0 to 10 and y from 0 to 5000. Draw the region corresponding to the inequality in part (b). (Shade out the unwanted region.)

(d) Mark a point on your diagram for each of these journeys and say whether the salesperson would be allowed to hire a car.

(i) Ms Jones, who wants a car for 3 days to do 500 miles

(ii) Mr Black, who needs to cover 1500 miles in 6 days

(iii) Ms Fortune, who needs to cover 1350 miles in 5 days

10.3 If $p + q = 8$ and $3p + 4q = 31$, work out the values of

(a) $4p + 4q$ (b) $4p + 5q$ (c) $2p + 3q$ (d) $p + 2q$

10.4 If $r + 3s = 19$ and $5r + s = 18$, work out the values of

(a) $6r + 4s$ (b) $3r + 2s$ (c) $15r + 3s$ (d) $14r$

10.5 Find the common solution of each of these pairs of equations.

(a) $a + b = 23$ (b) $5a + b = 15$ (c) $3x + 2y = 27$ (d) $3p - 2q = 28$
    $a - b = 5$ $3a + b = 7$ $x + 3y = 16$ $2p + 5q = 25$

10.6 Two school parties visited the zoo. The first party, consisting of 13 children and 3 adults, paid £27. The second party, consisting of 19 children and 5 adults, paid £41. What were the entrance fees for an adult and for a child? (There were no special rates for groups.)

10.7 This diagram, which is not drawn accurately, shows the lines whose equations are

$x - y = 3$, $x + 2y = 12$ and $4x - 7y = 18$.

Calculate the coordinates of A, B and C.

10.8 In this pair of linear equations, a stands for a number.

$$x + 2y = 5$$
$$3x + 6y = a$$

What can you say about the solution of the equations

(a) when $a = 10$ (b) when $a = 15$

10.9 Draw axes with x and y from $^-5$ to 5.
Draw the line $2x - 3y = 6$. Indicate the region $2x - 3y < 6$ by shading out the unwanted part.

10.10 (a) State a pair of inequalities which together describe the region left unshaded in this diagram.

(b) Calculate the coordinates of the point A.

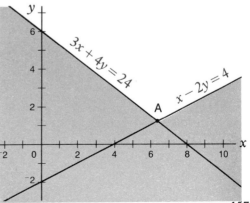

11 Graphs and functions

11.1 Karl is learning how to change the tyre on a wheel of a car.
As he does the job more and more often, he gets faster at it.
But eventually he gets to a point where he cannot do it any faster.

Sketch a graph showing how the time he takes to change a tyre
is related to the number of times he has done the job.
Draw axes like these.

Time taken
to change
a tyre

Number of times he has done the job

11.2 This sketch graph shows the amount of petrol in a car's tank
during a journey.

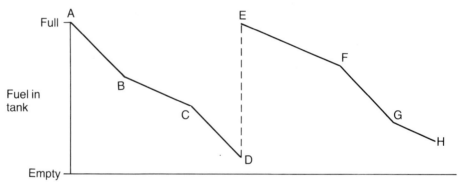

Distance travelled

The journey involved two kinds of driving: in towns and on main roads.
In towns the car does fewer miles to a gallon than on main roads.

(a) Which parts of the graph show driving in towns? Explain how
you decide.

(b) What does the dotted line DE show?

11.3 A boy leans out of a balcony and throws a ball upwards.
The height of the ball above the ground is given by the formula
$h = 25 + 20t - 5t^2$, where t is the time in seconds since the ball
was thrown and h is the height of the ball above the ground, in metres.

(a) Draw a graph of (t, h) for values of t from 0 to 5.
(b) Use the graph to find the length of time for which the ball
was higher than 30 m above the ground.

11.4 For each graph shown below, write down
(i) its gradient (ii) its intercept on the y-axis (iii) its equation

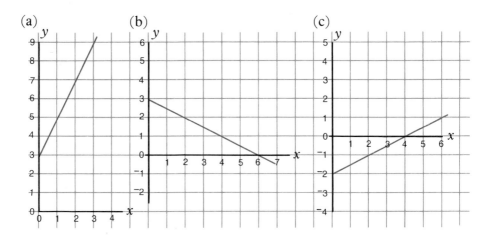

11.5 Draw axes with x and y from $^-5$ to 5.
(a) At each of these points, mark the value of $2x - 7y$ at that point:
$(0, 1)$, $(4, 1)$, $(2, 4)$, $(7, 3)$.
(b) Draw the line $2x - 7y = ^-7$.
(c) What is the gradient of the line?
(d) What is its intercept on the y-axis?
(e) Write down its equation, in the form $y = ax + b$.
(f) Use algebra to re-write the equation $2x - 7y = ^-7$ in the
form $y = ax + b$ and check that your answer agrees with
the answer to part (e).

11.6 The electrical resistance of a piece of wire increases as its
temperature increases.
A student did an experiment to investigate the relationship
between resistance and temperature. Here are her results.

T (temperature in °C)	20	30	50	70	80	100
R (resistance in ohms)	25·0	26·1	27·8	30·2	30·9	33

(a) Draw axes with T across (1 cm to 10 °C) and R up (1 cm
to 5 ohms). Plot the six points from the table.

(b) Draw a straight 'line of best fit' through the points. Find its
gradient and its intercept on the R-axis.

(c) Write the equation of your line of best fit.

11.7 Let s stand for the function $x \rightarrow 5 - 3x$.
(a) Calculate (i) s(3) (ii) s(0) (iii) s($^-4$)
(b) For which value of x is $s(x) = 20$?
(c) For which value of x is $s(x) = x$?

11.8 t is the function $x \to (x+1)(x-5)$.

(a) Copy and complete this table of values of t(x).

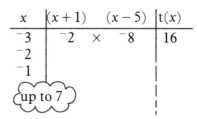

x	$(x+1)$		$(x-5)$	$t(x)$
$^-3$	$^-2$	$\times$	$^-8$	16
$^-2$				
$^-1$				

up to 7

(b) Draw a graph of t(x).

(c) Use the graph to answer this question: between which two values of x is $(x+1)(x-5)<5$?

(d) What are the two values of x for which $(x+1)(x-5)=0$?

(e) Explain how you can work out the values of x for which $(x+1)(x-5)=0$ without drawing a graph.

11.9 Work out where the graph of $x \to (x-2)(x-6)$ crosses the x-axis.

11.10 Where does each of these graphs cross the x-axis?

(a) $x \to x(x-4)$ (b) $x \to (x+3)(x+10)$ (c) $x \to (x-1)(x+5)$

11.11 Which of the drawings below could be a sketch of the graph of

(a) $y = \dfrac{x^2}{2}$ (b) $y = 5 - \dfrac{x}{2}$ (c) $y = \dfrac{2}{x}$ (d) $y = \dfrac{x}{2}$

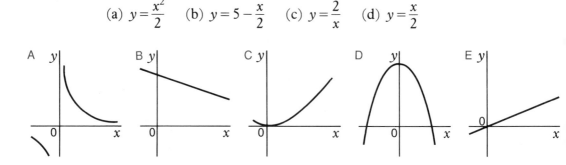

11.12 The values of p and q in this table are believed to fit an equation of the form $q = a\sqrt{p} + b$.

p	0·8	1·8	2·3	3·6	5·5	8·9
q	14·5	16·7	17·6	19·5	21·7	24·9

(a) Make a new table of values of $\sqrt{p}$ and q.

(b) Draw a graph and from it find a and b.

11.13 The values of r and s in this table are believed to fit roughly an equation of the form $s = ar^2 + b$.

r	0·6	1·1	1·5	2·0	2·3	2·5
s	17·5	16·2	14·6	12·0	10·1	8·6

By drawing a suitable graph, find values for a and b.

11.14 This graph shows the speed of a coach as it slows down to a stop. Calculate approximately the distance travelled during the 10 seconds shown on the graph, and describe your method of calculation.

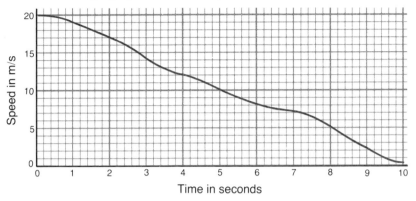

12 Proportionality

12.1 A shop sells silver braid. The cost of the braid is proportional to the length bought. You can buy 40 cm for £1·00.

(a) What will be the cost of   (i) 120 cm   (ii) 30 cm   (iii) 90 cm
(b) How much braid will you get for   (i) £5   (ii) £2·50   (iii) £25

12.2 Two towers stand side by side.
One tower is 32·5 m high and casts a shadow 45·1 m long.
The second tower's shadow is 58·3 m long.

(a) Calculate the multiplier from the first shadow to the second shadow.

(b) Calculate the height of the second tower, to the nearest 0·1 m.

12.3 A firm sells copper tubing of diameter 2·0 cm. The weight of a piece of this tubing is proportional to its length, and the cost is also proportional to the length.
A piece 30 cm long weighs 250 g and costs 48p.

(a) Calculate the weight and the cost of a 50 cm piece.
(b) What length can you buy for £10?

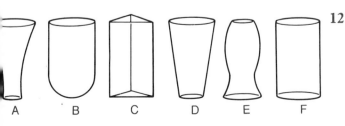

12.4 In which of these containers will the volume of liquid be proportional to depth?

12.5 A student studying electricity varied the voltage across a piece of wire and measured the current in the wire each time. Here are her results. V stands for the voltage, in volts, and I for the current, in amps.

V	1·5	2·2	3·2	4·3	5·0
I	3·9	5·7	8·3	11·2	13·0

(a) Draw axes with V across and I up. Plot the five points, and draw the graph of (V, I).
(b) Is I proportional to V? How can you tell from the graph?
(c) Find the gradient of the graph.
(d) Write down the equation connecting I and V in the form $I = \ldots V$.

12.6 Find the equation connecting y and x for each of these graphs.

12.7 A van which travels at an average speed of 27 m.p.h. can cover the distance from London to Barnsley in $6\frac{1}{2}$ hours.

(a) What is the average speed of a coach which can do the same trip in $3\frac{1}{4}$ hours?
(b) How long would the journey take in a veteran car with an average speed of 9 m.p.h.?

12.8 If a beam of a certain cross-section is supported at both ends, the weight, W kg, it can carry at its centre is inversely proportional to its length, l cm.

If $W = 1·6$ when $l = 25$, calculate

(a) W when $l = 12·5$ (b) W when $l = 40$ (c) l when $W = 2·5$

12.9 The weight, W kg, which can be supported by a certain kind of rope is proportional to the square of its diameter, d mm.
When d is 12, then W is 2500. Calculate, to 2 s.f.,
(a) W when $d = 22$ (b) W when $d = 10$

13 Exponential growth and decay

13.1 When Sadia was born, several relatives gave money for her, amounting to £50 altogether. Sadia's mother put the money into a savings account where the rate of interest was 8% p.a. On Sadia's 18th birthday, her mother told her about the account. Calculate the amount in the account by then.

13.2 An oven is switched off, opened, and allowed to cool.
The temperature afterwards is given by the formula $T = 15 + 200 \times 4^{-t}$.
T stands for the temperature in °C, and t for the time in minutes since the oven was switched off.

    (a) Calculate T when t is 0, 1, 2, 3 and 4.

    (b) Draw a graph of (t, T). What happens to T as t increases?

14 Sequences and iteration

14.1 The nth term of a sequence a is given by the formula $a_n = \dfrac{n(n+1)}{2}$.

    (a) Write down the values of a_1, a_2, a_3, a_4, a_5 and a_6.
    (b) What name is given to this sequence?

14.2 Find a formula for the nth term of the arithmetic sequence $3, 7, 11, 15, \ldots$

14.3 The sequence u is an arithmetic sequence. $u_1 = 5$ and $u_2 = 11$.
    (a) Write down the value of u_3.
    (b) Find a formula for u_n in terms of n.

14.4 This pattern of short and tall houses continues along a street. Find a formula for the number of the nth tall house.

14.5 Find a formula for the nth term of the geometric sequence $3, 12, 48, 192, \ldots$

14.6 (a) Write down the values of d_1 to d_6 produced by this flowchart.

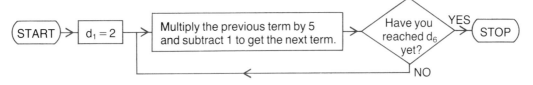

    (b) Write down the formula connecting d_n and d_{n+1}.

14.7 v is a sequence whose first term v_1 is 8. The formula connecting v_n and v_{n+1} is $v_{n+1} = 2v_n + 3$. Write down the values of v_2, v_3, v_4 and v_5.

14.8 The sequence d starts $3, 8, 23, 68, \ldots$ The formula connecting d_n and d_{n+1} is of the form $d_{n+1} = ad_n + b$. Find a and b.

163

14.9 Let r_n be the number of dots in the nth 'ring' of dots in this diagram.
(For example, $r_1 = 4$ and $r_2 = 12$.)

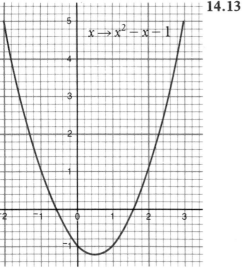

4 3 2 1

(a) Find the formula connecting r_n and r_{n+1}.

(b) Find the formula for r_n in terms of n.

14.10 The iteration formula for a sequence u is $u_{n+1} = \dfrac{3u_n + 1}{2}$.

(a) Starting with $u_1 = 5$, calculate u_2, u_3, u_4 and u_5.
(b) Does the sequence appear to converge when $u_1 = 5$?
(c) Calculate the fixed point of the iteration formula (the value of u_1 for which $u_1 = u_2 = u_3 = u_4 = \ldots$).

14.11 The iteration formula for a sequence u is $u_{n+1} = \dfrac{3u_n + 1}{5}$.

(a) Starting with $u_1 = 1$, calculate u_2, u_3, u_4 and u_5.
(b) Does the sequence appear to converge when $u_1 = 1$?
(c) Calculate the fixed point of the iteration formula.

14.12 x is a fixed point of the iteration formula $u_{n+1} = \dfrac{3}{u_n - 2}$.

(a) Show that x satisfies the equation $x^2 - 2x - 3 = 0$.
(b) Solve this equation by factorisation to find the possible values of x.

14.13 This graph of the function $x \rightarrow x^2 - x - 1$ shows that there is a solution of the equation $x^2 - x - 1 = 0$ near to $^-0{\cdot}6$ and another one near to $1{\cdot}6$.

$x \rightarrow x^2 - x - 1$

(a) Show that the equation $x^2 - x - 1 = 0$ can be written $x = \dfrac{1}{x - 1}$.

(b) This equation can be made into an iteration formula $u_{n+1} = \dfrac{1}{u_n - 1}$.
Starting with $u_1 = 1{\cdot}6$, calculate u_2, u_3, etc. and see if the sequence converges.

If not, start again with $u_1 = {}^-0{\cdot}6$.

Either way, find one of the solutions of the equation $x^2 - x - 1 = 0$, correct to 2 d.p.

(c) Re-arrange the equation $x^2 - x - 1 = 0$ in a different way (but still in the form $x = \ldots$). Write down the corresponding iteration formula, and see if it leads to the other solution. If not, try another arrangement.

15 Loci

15.1 This is a plan of a back garden, drawn to a scale of $\frac{1}{2}$ cm to 1 m.

Copy the plan and colour the part of the garden which cannot be seen from the window.

15.2 Two farmers living at A and B agree to dig a well and share it.

The well must be the same distance from A and from B, but it must be dug on land no higher than 10 m above sea-level.

(a) Trace or copy the map and show the possible positions of the well.

(b) Mark with a W the position which is closest to the farmhouses.

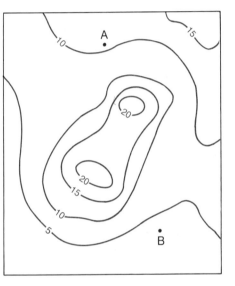

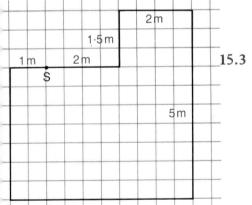

15.3 The plan on the left shows a room with only one electric socket (S).

A standard lamp has a lead which is 3 m long. Draw the room plan to scale and shade the area where you could put the lamp and be able to plug it in.

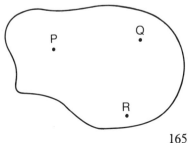

15.4 This is an island with three schools P, Q and R. Children living on the island go to the nearest school.

Draw the map and divide the island up between the three schools. Which school serves the largest area?

16 Pythagoras' rule

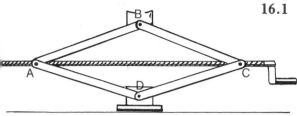

16.1 This diagram shows a type of car jack. When the handle is turned, the points A and C move closer together, and the point B rises.

The lengths AB, BC, CD and DA are each 15 cm. Calculate the height of B above D when AC is 22 cm.

16.2 The three corners of a triangle are at A (1, 0), B (7, 3) and C (3, 8). Calculate the length of   (a) AB   (b) BC   (c) CA

17 The circle: circumference and area

17.1 This is an old photograph of the Giant Wheel in Vienna.

(a) How many cars are there round the edge of the wheel?

(b) Each car is about 2·5 m tall, and hangs from a pivot.

From the photo, estimate the distance between pivots.

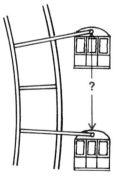

(c) Use your estimate in (b) to estimate the circumference of the wheel.

(d) Hence estimate the diameter of the wheel.

17.2 Calculate these. Give each answer correct to 3 s.f.

(a) The area of a circle of radius 6·55 m

(b) The circumference of a circle of radius 2·93 m

(c) The radius of a circle of area 0·85 m²

(d) The area of a circle of circumference 13·7 m

17.3 A circular saw is rotating at a speed of 100 revolutions per minute. The diameter of the saw is 35 cm.

(a) How far does a point on the edge of the saw travel in one minute?

(b) Calculate the speed of a point on the edge of the saw, in cm/s, to the nearest 10 cm/s.

18 Angle relationships

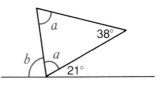

18.1 The angles marked a in this diagram are equal. Calculate a and b.

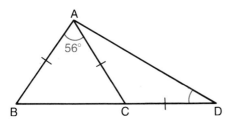

18.2 In the diagram on the left AB = AC = CD.

Calculate the angle marked x.

Explain each step of your working.

18.3 ABC is a triangle
The side BC is extended to form the **exterior angle** at C (marked x).

Explain why $x = a + b$.

(You may find it helpful to add an extra line through C, parallel to BA, as shown below.)

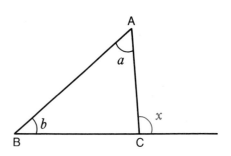

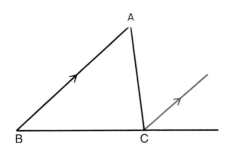

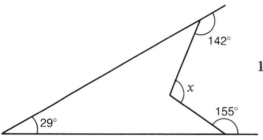

18.4 Show that, in the diagram on the left,

$$a + b = c + d.$$

18.5 This diagram shows part of a regular polygon.

How many sides does the polygon have?

160°

18.6 Calculate the angle marked x in the diagram on the left.

Explain each step of your working.

142°

x

155°

29°

19 Mappings and symmetry

19.1 Which of these 'words' have a 2-fold rotation centre?

(a) pod   (b) shoys   (c) bozzop   (d) onzuo

(e) dollop   (f) hoxoy   (g) poqdob   (h) snous

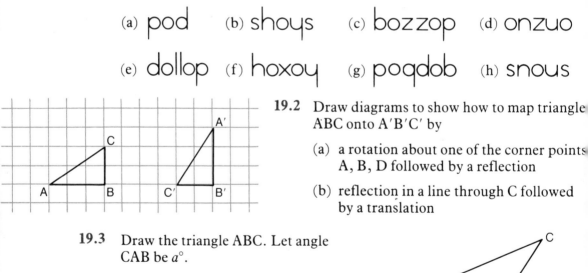

A'

C

A   B   C'   B'

19.2 Draw diagrams to show how to map triangle ABC onto A'B'C' by

(a) a rotation about one of the corner points A, B, D followed by a reflection

(b) reflection in a line through C followed by a translation

19.3 Draw the triangle ABC. Let angle CAB be $a°$.

(a) Reflect the triangle in the line AB. Draw the image and label it AB'C'.

C

A $a°$ B

(b) Rotate triangle AB'C' through $a°$ anticlockwise about A. Draw the image and label it AB"C".

(c) Which single mapping maps ABC directly onto AB"C"? Describe it as precisely as you can.

20 Trigonometry

20.1 Calculate the lengths marked with letters. (All measurements in cm.)

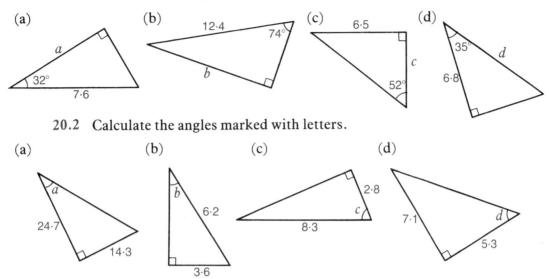

(a) (b) (c) (d)

20.2 Calculate the angles marked with letters.

(a) (b) (c) (d)

20.3 A straight roadway is 10·4 m wide. If you walk across it at an angle of 35° to an edge of the roadway, how far do you walk?

20.4 The diagram on the right shows the symmetrical cross-section of a railway embankment.

Calculate the angle which each sloping edge makes with the horizontal.

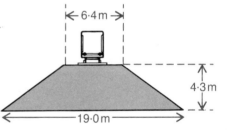

20.5 A microphone is hung from the sides of a school hall, as shown in this drawing.

(a) Calculate the angle which each of the two wires makes with the horizontal.

(b) Calculate the height of the microphone above the floor of the hall.

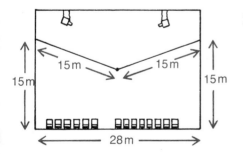

20.6 (a) Find two values of θ in the range 0° to 360° for which sin θ = 0·4. (Give each angle to the nearest 0·1°.)

(b) Find two values of θ in the range 0° to 360° for which cos θ = ⁻0·8.

20.7 (a) Sketch on the same axes the graphs of θ → sin θ and θ → cos θ for values of θ from 0° to 360°.

(b) For which values of θ between 0° and 360° is sin θ equal to cos θ?

169

21 Three dimensions

21.1 A child's toy consists of a solid block of wood with four wheels. Here are a side elevation and a front elevation of the toy, drawn to a scale of 1 cm to 10 cm.

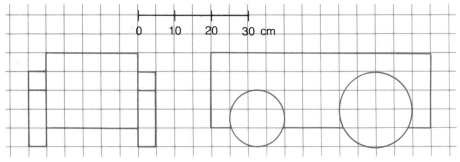

Draw, to the same scale, a plan view of the toy.

21.2 Copy this perspective drawing. (Your copy does not have to be exact.)

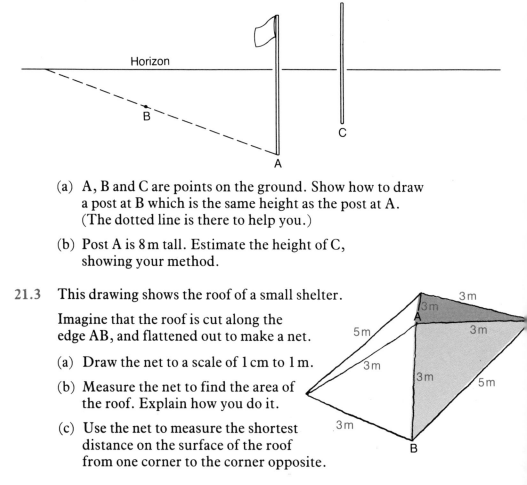

(a) A, B and C are points on the ground. Show how to draw a post at B which is the same height as the post at A. (The dotted line is there to help you.)

(b) Post A is 8 m tall. Estimate the height of C, showing your method.

21.3 This drawing shows the roof of a small shelter.

Imagine that the roof is cut along the edge AB, and flattened out to make a net.

(a) Draw the net to a scale of 1 cm to 1 m.

(b) Measure the net to find the area of the roof. Explain how you do it.

(c) Use the net to measure the shortest distance on the surface of the roof from one corner to the corner opposite.

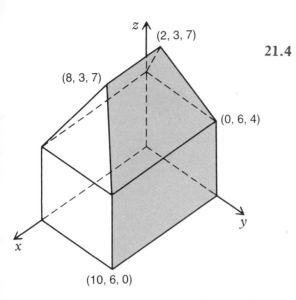

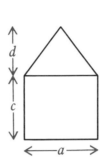

21.4 The diagram on the left shows a house. All measurements are in metres.

The diagrams below show two elevations of the house.

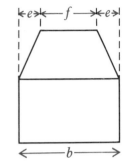

(a) Work out the lengths marked a, b, c, d, e and f.

(b) The 'roof-space' of the house can be divided into three sections, A, B and C, as shown in this diagram.

If part B is removed, and parts A and C are moved together so that the red triangles coincide, what kind of solid will A and C together make?

(c) Calculate the **total** volume of the roof-space, showing your method clearly.

[Volume of pyramid $= \frac{1}{3} \times$ area of base $\times$ height.]

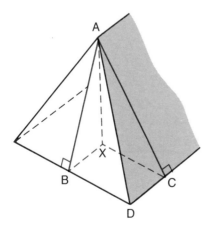

21.5 The diagram on the left shows an end of the same roof as shown above.

(a) Calculate AB.

(b) Calculate AC.

(c) Calculate AD.

(d) Calculate the **total area** of the roof of the house, showing your method clearly.

(e) Calculate the angle which the sloping edge AD makes with the horizontal.

21.6 The helix shown here divides the curved surface of the cylinder into two parts, black and white.
(a) Calculate the area of the black part.
(b) Calculate the length of the helix.

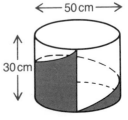

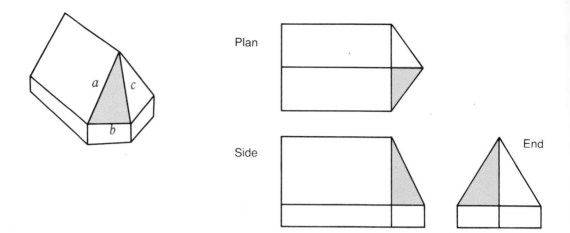

Plan

Side

End

21.7 These drawings show a sketch and three views of a tent. One triangular panel is shown shaded. Its edges are a, b and c.

Make rough copies of the three views.

In which view does edge a appear correctly to scale, so that you could measure its length from the view? Mark the edge with an a in that view. Then do the same for edge b and edge c.

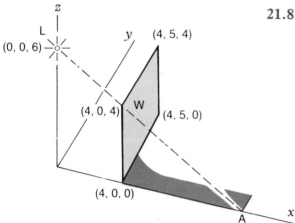

21.8 A light is situated at L. The vertical wall W casts a shadow on the horizontal ground.

Part of the shadow is shown. A is one corner of it.

(a) What are the coordinates of A?

(b) Find the coordinates of the other corner(s) of the shadow.

22 The Earth

22.1 This is part of a map on which lines of latitude and longitude are shown equally spaced.

(a) Write down the latitude and longitude of each marked point.

(b) Calculate the distance in km from E to D, taking the radius of the Earth as 6370 km.

(c) Calculate the distance from A to F.

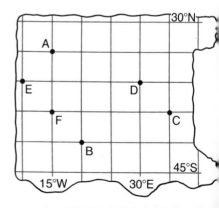

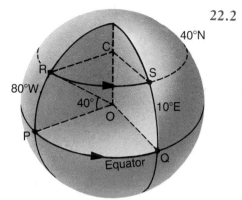

22.2 P and Q are points on the equator with longitudes 80°W and 10°E.

R and S are points on the 40°N circle of latitude, with the same longitudes as P and Q.

Take the length of the equator as 40 000 km.

(a) What is the angle POQ?

(b) Calculate the distance from P to Q along the equator.

(c) The radius of the 40°N circle of latitude is cos 40° times the radius of the Earth.

Use this fact to calculate the distance RS measured along the circle of latitude.

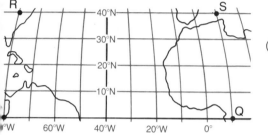

(d) The map on the left shows P, Q, R and S. Is the distance RS along the parallel of latitude shown correctly in relation to the distance RS along the equator? If not, is RS too small or too large in relation to PQ?

23 Enlargement and reduction

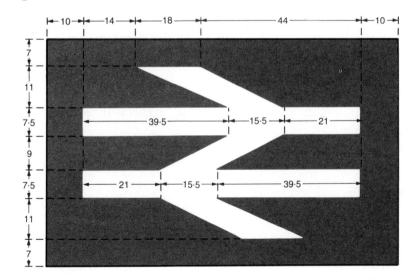

23.1 The dimensions on this drawing are in millimetres. Suppose the drawing is enlarged so that the red rectangle is 144 mm high.

(a) Calculate the scale factor of the enlargement.
(b) How long will the red rectangle be in the enlargement?
(c) How long and how wide will each horizontal bar be?

23.2 A church council has commissioned a sculptor to make a stone statue of an angel. The statue is to be painted gold. The sculptor has made a model of the statue, also in stone. The model is 25 cm high, weighs 6·4 kg and needs 0·15 litre of gold paint.

The real statue is to be 2·0 metres high.

(a) How much will the real statue weigh?
(b) How much gold paint will be needed to paint it?

23.3 Blagdon Zoo covers an area of 85 500 m². Inside the zoo is a model zoo. The model is a model of Blagdon Zoo itself, and is made to a scale of 2 cm to 1 m.

(a) Calculate the area of the model zoo, in m².
(b) Inside the model zoo is a model of the model zoo. Calculate the area of this model, in cm².

24 Vector geometry

24.1 In this diagram, OACB is a parallelogram. B is the midpoint of AD.
$\overrightarrow{OA} = \underset{\sim}{a}$ and $\overrightarrow{OB} = \underset{\sim}{b}$.

Express each of these vectors in terms of $\underset{\sim}{a}$ and $\underset{\sim}{b}$.

(a) $\overrightarrow{OC}$ (b) $\overrightarrow{AB}$ (c) $\overrightarrow{AD}$ (d) $\overrightarrow{OD}$ (e) $\overrightarrow{DC}$

24.2 In this diagram, $\overrightarrow{OC} = 3\underset{\sim}{a}$ and $\overrightarrow{OD} = 2\underset{\sim}{b}$.

E is the midpoint of AD.

F is $\frac{1}{4}$ of the way along DC.

(a) Express in terms of $\underset{\sim}{a}$ and $\underset{\sim}{b}$
   (i) $\overrightarrow{AD}$ (ii) $\overrightarrow{AE}$ (iii) $\overrightarrow{OE}$

(b) Express in terms of $\underset{\sim}{a}$ and $\underset{\sim}{b}$
   (i) $\overrightarrow{DC}$ (ii) $\overrightarrow{DF}$ (iii) $\overrightarrow{OF}$

(c) What is the relation between $\overrightarrow{OF}$ and $\overrightarrow{OE}$? Give the reason for your answer.

25 Statistics

25.1 A firm sells paper clips in boxes marked 'about 100'. To check the contents, a sample of 20 boxes were opened and the clips counted.

Number of clips in box	95	96	97	98	99	100	101	102
Number of boxes	1	2	4	4	7	1	0	1

Calculate the mean number of paper clips per box in the sample.

25.2 Large samples of two species of snake were caught and the length of each snake was measured. The cumulative frequency graphs of the lengths in each species (A and B) are shown below.

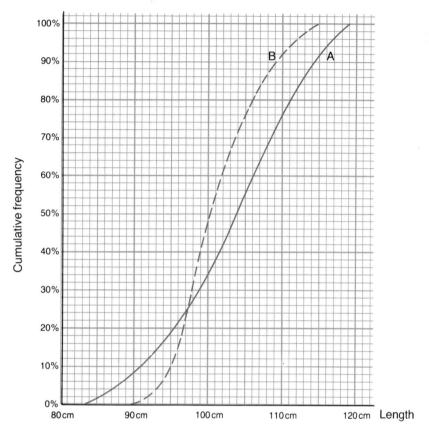

(a) What is the range of lengths in each species?

(b) What is the median length in each species?

(c) What percentage of species A were more than 1 metre in length?

(d) What percentage of species B were more than 1 metre in length?

(e) Calculate the interquartile range of each species.

(f) If you compare the interquartile ranges, what does that tell you about the distribution of lengths in the two species?

(g) Copy and complete this percentage frequency table.

(h) From the information in your table, draw two frequency charts, one for each species. Lay them out on the page so that they can easily be compared.

Length in cm	Percentage of species A	Percentage of species B
80–85	2%	0%
85–90	7%	0%
90–95	10%	10%
⋮	⋮	⋮
115–120		

25.3 Two wine 'experts' were asked to rate the quality of 15 different types of wine and to give each wine a score out of 10. Here are their scores.

Wine	A	B	C	D	E	F	G	H	I	J	K	L	M	N	O
1st expert	6	4	6	3	8	1	8	8	9	4	2	5	4	3	7
2nd expert	8	3	6	4	9	2	1	8	8	4	3	5	5	3	6

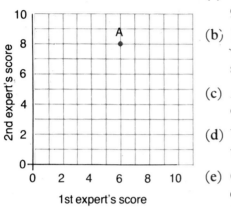

(a) Draw axes as shown on the left. Mark each pair of scores as a point on the diagram.

(b) Look at the diagram. Is there any particular wine which the experts disagree about very strongly? If so, which wine is it?

(c) Apart from this wine, is there a reasonable amount of agreement between the experts?

(d) Where would the points lie if the experts agreed on the score for every one of the wines?

(e) Calculate the mean of the scores given by the first expert. Do the same for the second expert. Which expert gave higher scores on average?

(f) The magazine which asked the experts to rate the wines wants to print an 'order of merit', showing the 15 wines in order of quality, best first. Suggest how they might make an 'order of merit'.

26 Selections and arrangements

26.1 A salesman starts from town S and goes on a tour, visiting each of the other towns once. One possible order for visiting them is CADB. How many different possible orders are there?

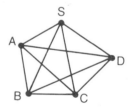

26.2 Stevie's Jeans are made in these waist measurements

26 28 30 32 34 36 38

and in these inside leg measurements

27 29 31 33

(a) The factory makes jeans with every different possible combination of measurements, e.g. waist 38, inside leg 29.
How many possible combinations are there?

(b) Stevie's decide to include a waist measurement of 40 in their range and also an inside leg measurement of 25.
They manufacture every possible combination **except** waist 40 with inside leg 25. How many possible combinations are there?

26.3 A, B, C, D, E, F, G and H are eight people. B, C and G are friendly with each other. A is friendly with D, with E and with H. F is friendly with B, D, E and H.

Can all eight people sit in a row so that every person sits next to a friend?

If not, can they do it if one person drops out? If so, who could drop out, and who could sit at each end?

27 Probability

27.1 Audrey has five cards, numbered 1, 2, 3, 4, 5. She shuffles them and Kevin picks two cards at random.

(a) Make a list of all the possible pairs of cards Kevin could pick.

(b) What is the probability that Kevin picks a pair of consecutive numbers (e.g. 1 and 2, or 3 and 4, etc.)?

27.2 Calculate the probability of throwing four sixes in four throws of an ordinary dice.

27.3 Square sheets of plastic are fed into two cutting machines, one after the other. The first machine is supposed to cut each sheet in half 'across' and the second to cut in half 'down'.

The machines are independent of each other, but both are unreliable. It has been observed that the first machine fails to cut 1 sheet in 5, and the second fails to cut 1 sheet in 4.

If a sheet is fed into the machines, calculate the probability that it comes out   (a) not cut at all   (b) cut into halves   (c) cut into quarters

27.4 Stephanie has invented a game for Simon to play. Simon throws three coins. If they all land the same way (all heads or all tails) Stephanie pays Simon 10p. If they are not all the same, Simon throws them all again. This time if they are all the same, Stephanie pays him 5p. Otherwise he pays Stephanie 10p.

(a) Copy this tree diagram and write the probabilities on the branches.

(b) Calculate the probability that Simon
    (i) wins 10p
    (ii) wins 5p
    (iii) loses 10p

Coins same (Simon wins 10p.)

Same (Simon wins 5p.)

Coins not same

Not same (Simon loses 10p.)

(c) Simon plays 1000 times. About how much do you expect him to win or lose altogether?

M Miscellaneous questions

The questions in this section are taken from the SMP 11–16 pilot 16+ examination (papers 3 and 4) and are reprinted with the kind permission of the Oxford and Cambridge Schools Examination Board, and the East Anglian Examinations Board.

M1 Work out $\dfrac{43 \cdot 76 \times 0 \cdot 0163}{\sqrt{283 \cdot 71}}$.

(a) Write down all the figures in your calculator display.

(b) Write your answer to 3 significant figures.

M2 The speed of light in space is 299 800 000 m/s, to 4 significant figures.

Write this number in standard index form.

M3 Find the value of x if $\dfrac{450}{x} = 15$.

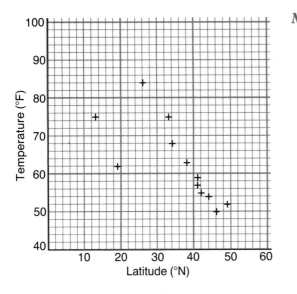

M4 The maximum temperature in degrees Fahrenheit (°F) is recorded on a November day in twelve places in North America.

These temperatures are marked on this scatter diagram, together with the latitude of each place.

(The latitude, measured in degrees, tells you how far north a place is from the equator.)

What can you say about the relationship between latitude and temperature?

M5 Draw axes with x and y from $^-4$ to 10.
Draw a straight line through $(^-4, \, ^-3)$ and $(8, 3)$.

(a) What is the gradient of this line?

(b) Write down the equation of the line.

M6 Which of these is the smallest?
(a) 2^{16} (b) 4^8 (c) 8^4 (d) 16^2

178

M7 A 'penny farthing' bicycle has wheels
of two different sizes.

Their diameters are 125 cm and 39·5 cm.

(a) Calculate the circumference of

  (i) the large wheel   (ii) the small wheel

(b) How far does the cycle travel as the
large wheel makes 20 revolutions?
Give your answer in **metres**.

(c) How many revolutions does the small
wheel make in travelling the same
distance?

M8 A piston fits tightly in a vertical cylinder, trapping the air
below it.

When a weight w kg is placed on the piston, the height of the
piston above the base is h m.

h is inversely proportional to w.

(a) Sketch a graph of (w, h) on axes like these.

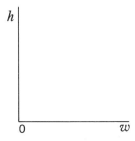

(b) What happens to h when w is halved?

(c) If $h = 45$ when $w = 250$, calculate h when $w = 300$.

M9 I travel to school by bus. Sometimes the bus arrives at the bus stop
at the same time as I do. At other times I have to wait, for up to
10 minutes.

If the traffic lights are all green, the bus journey takes 7 minutes.
Usually the journey takes longer, sometimes as long as 12 minutes.

It takes me 5 minutes to walk from home to the bus stop. It takes me
2 minutes to walk from the bus into school. I have to be in school
by 8:45 a.m.

(a) By what time must I leave home to be **sure** of arriving at school
on time?

(b) If I leave home at this time, what is the earliest I could arrive
at school?

M10 (a) Write down the sum of the interior angles of a quadrilateral.

(b) Draw this pentagon.
Draw a diagonal in it.

Work out the sum of the interior
angles of the pentagon.

(c) Suppose that two of the interior angles of a pentagon are each 120°
and the other three angles are all equal to each other.
Work out the size of each of the other three angles.

M11 The frequency of a note played on the E-string of a violin
is **inversely** proportional to the length of
the vibrating part of the string.

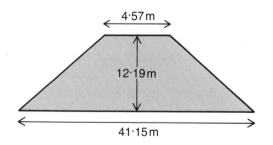

(a) What happens to the frequency of the note when
the length of the vibrating part of the string is halved?

(b) Frequency is measured in hertz (Hz).
When the vibrating length is 204 mm, the frequency is 2048 Hz.
(i) Calculate the frequency when the length is 250 mm.
(ii) Calculate the length when the frequency is 3000 Hz.

M12 This diagram shows a cross-section of a symmetrical railway
embankment. It is in the shape of a trapezium.
The diagram is not to scale.

4·57 m

12·19 m

41·15 m

(a) (i) Calculate the area of the cross-section.

(ii) How many cubic metres of material are required to build
a 100 m length of the embankment?

(b) This is a drawing of the
same cross-section.

(i) Calculate the length AB.

(ii) Calculate the angle θ.

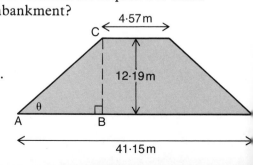

When measuring skid marks, the police can use this formula
to estimate the speed of the vehicle.

$$s = \sqrt{(30fd)}$$

s is the speed in miles per hour (m.p.h.).
d is the length of the skid, in feet.
f is a number which depends on the weather and the type of road.

This table shows some values of f.

		Road surface	
		Concrete	Tar
Weather	Wet	0·4	0·5
	Dry	0·8	1·0

(a) A car travelling on a wet concrete road makes a skid mark
of length 80 feet. How fast was it travelling?

(b) (i) When the road surface is tar and the weather is dry, the
formula may be written

$$s = \sqrt{(30d)}$$

Complete this table to show the values of s for the given
values of d, to 1 decimal place.

d	50	100	150	200	250
$30d$	1500				
$s = \sqrt{(30d)}$	38·7				

(ii) Draw axes, with d from 0 to 250 (use 2 cm for 50) and
s from 0 to 100 (use 1 cm for 10).
Draw the graph of (d, s).

(iii) Use your graph to find how many feet a car would skid on
a dry tar road at 75 m.p.h.

M14 In this question, you will need the formula

Surface area of disc $= 2\pi r(r + t)$

where r is the radius and t the thickness.

The disease *multiple mycloma* causes
the red blood cells, which are like discs,
to stick together (like a pile of coins).

When the cells stick together, there are
fewer faces to absorb oxygen.

1 cell

4 cells stuck
together

The cells have a thickness of $2\cdot2$ microns
and a diameter of $7\cdot2$ microns.

The surface area is measured in
square microns.

(a)   (i) What is the radius of a cell?

     (ii) Find the surface area of one cell.

     (iii) Find the total surface area
         of four separate cells.

(b)   (i) Find the surface area of four
         cells stuck together.

     (ii) Find the percentage decrease in surface area when four cells
         stick together.

M15 Work out $(4\cdot29 \times 10^{-7}) \times (2\cdot79 \times 10^{3})$.
Give your answer (a) in standard index form
                   (b) in ordinary decimal form

M16 This table gives the first four terms of a sequence u.

u_1	u_2	u_3	u_4	...
3	6	12	24	...

(a) There is a simple relationship connecting each term with the next on
What is the relationship? Write it in words or in symbols.

(b) Write down a formula for the nth term u_n in terms of n.

M17 For cars travelling at normal speed, the air drag is roughly
proportional to SV^2, where S is the surface area of the car
and V is the speed.

By what number will the air drag be multiplied when the car
increases speed from $40\,$km/h to $120\,$km/h?

M18 Opticians use the formula $D = \dfrac{1}{u} + \dfrac{1}{v}$.

What can you say about the value of D if $v = 0\cdot02$ and u is approximately $1\,000\,000$?

M19 Solve the equation $x^2 - 3x - 10 = 0$.

M20 The mean weight of eight oarsmen is $78\cdot3\,\text{kg}$.
The ninth member of the crew weighs $48\cdot6\,\text{kg}$.

What is the mean weight of all nine?

M21 A vacuum pump is designed to remove 25% of the gas in a vacuum chamber with each stroke.

(a) What percentage of the gas will be left after
    (i) 1 stroke   (ii) 2 strokes

(b) How many strokes are needed to remove about 90% of the gas which was originally in the chamber?

M22 Roughly how many matchboxes of this size have a total volume of 1 cubic metre?

Show clearly how you get your estimate.

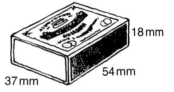

18mm

54mm

37mm

M23 A sequence begins $1, 3, 7, 15, 31, 63, \cdots$
It has a simple term-to-term rule.

(a) Write down this rule in words.

(b) Use the rule to find the next term of the sequence.

(c) The nth term of the sequence is denoted by s_n.
    Write the rule as an equation connecting s_{n+1} and s_n.

(d) Make a new sequence by adding 1 to each term of the sequence above.
    Write an expression in terms of n for the nth term of the new sequence.

(e) Use your answer to part (d) to write down a formula for s_n in terms of n.

M24 x and y are given by these formulas.

$$x = pt \quad \text{and} \quad y = p(1 + qt)$$

(a) Find a formula for y in terms of p, q and x which does not include t.

(b) Find a formula for x in terms of p, q and y which does not include t.

M25 (a) A bank exchanges £ sterling for dollars at the rate of $1·39 for £1.
It deducts 5% for doing the work.
How much in dollars will I get for £200?

(b) Dollars may be exchanged for £ sterling at the rate of
$1·41 for £1. Again the deduction is 5%.
How much in £ sterling will I get for $260?

M26 A salesman reports an increase of 55% in his sales this year
compared with last year.

The increase was £43 197.
What were his actual sales this year?

M27 The iteration formula of a sequence u is

$$u_{n+1} = \frac{u_n - 1}{4}$$

(a) Starting with $u_1 = 5$, calculate u_2, u_3, u_4, u_5 and u_6.

(b) Guess the value of the limit towards which the sequence
seems to converge.

(c) Calculate the fixed point of the iteration formula
(the value of u_1 for which $u_1 = u_2 = u_3$ etc.).

M28 $y \propto \dfrac{1}{x^2}$

$y = 1·8$ when $x = 4$.

Find y when $x = 12$.

M29 A hospital keeps two types of glucose solution, weak and strong.

The weak solution contains 20 g of glucose per litre.
The strong solution contains 80 g of glucose per litre.

(a) Suppose x litres of the weak solution are mixed with y litres of the
strong solution.

Write an expression, in terms of x and y, for

(i) the total volume of the mixture, in litres

(ii) the amount of glucose in the mixture, in grams

(b) A nurse needs to mix the weak and strong solutions to make
6 litres of a new solution, containing 45 g of glucose per litre.

Calculate the volume of weak solution and the volume of strong
solution which she must mix together.

M30 What is the straight-line distance between $(7, 5)$ and $(1, {}^-3)$?

M31 Butter is to be supplied to Hillbury's Superstore in boxes containing 250 g packs of butter.

Each 250 g pack is a cuboid measuring 96 mm by 64 mm by 36 mm.

The internal dimensions of the boxes into which these are to be packed are 500 mm by 300 mm by 250 mm.

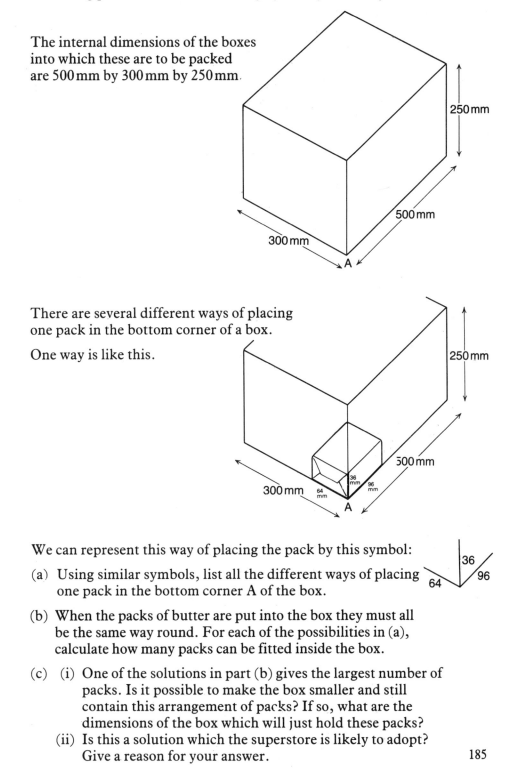

There are several different ways of placing one pack in the bottom corner of a box.

One way is like this.

We can represent this way of placing the pack by this symbol:

(a) Using similar symbols, list all the different ways of placing one pack in the bottom corner A of the box.

(b) When the packs of butter are put into the box they must all be the same way round. For each of the possibilities in (a), calculate how many packs can be fitted inside the box.

(c) (i) One of the solutions in part (b) gives the largest number of packs. Is it possible to make the box smaller and still contain this arrangement of packs? If so, what are the dimensions of the box which will just hold these packs?

   (ii) Is this a solution which the superstore is likely to adopt? Give a reason for your answer.

M32 The digits 1, 2, 3, 4, 5, 6, 7, 8, 9 are each printed on a separate card and the nine cards are shuffled.

A card is chosen at random, looked at, and replaced.
Then the pack is shuffled again and a second card is chosen at random.

The first number chosen forms the 'tens' digit of a number, the second the 'units' digit.
For example, if 5 and then 6 are chosen, the number formed is 56.

(a) What is the probability that a number less than 20 is formed?

(b) What is the probability that the number 14 is formed?

M33 The face of Brian's watch is decorated with two circles and a square.

The shaded part is gold.

One side of the square measures 20·0 mm.

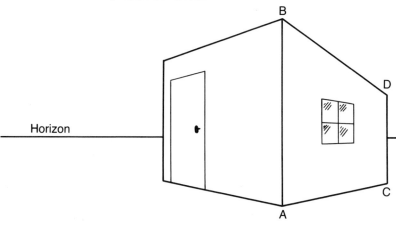

(a) What is the radius of the small circle?

(b) What is the area of gold?

(c) Calculate the radius of the large circle.

M34 Trace the diagram below, which is a perspective drawing of a 'lean-to' shed.

The height AB on the real shed is 2·4 m.

Estimate the height CD on the real shed.
Do not rub out any extra lines you add to your diagram.

Radius 40 cm

Radius 20 cm

70 cm   θ

d

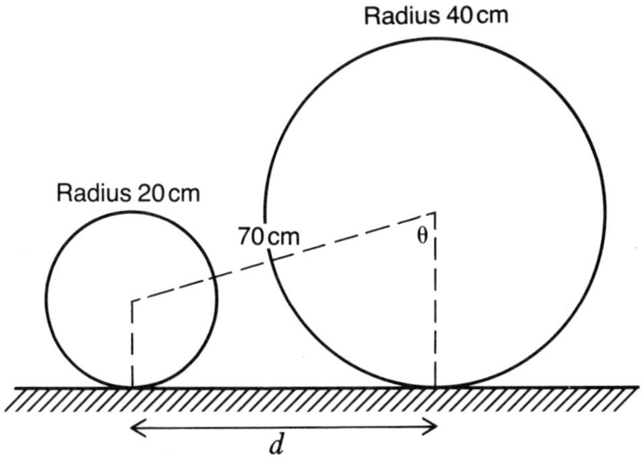

(a) This diagram shows two wheels, of radius 20 cm and 40 cm, standing on horizontal ground.

The distance between their centres is 70 cm.

(i) Calculate the distance marked d.

(ii) Calculate the angle marked θ.

(b) The same two wheels, with their centres still 70 cm apart, are connected by a tight belt, as shown below.

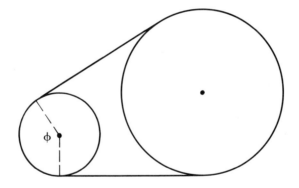

φ

(i) Draw the diagram and add the line of symmetry.

(ii) Calculate the angle φ to the nearest degree.

(iii) What fraction of the circumference of the smaller wheel is touching the belt?

(iv) Calculate the total length of the belt, showing all your working.

M36 (a) Factorise the expression $x^2 - x - 6$.

(b) Solve the equation $x^2 - x = 6$.

M37 Pauline and Quentin have inherited this plot of land.

(a) Calculate the area of the plot.

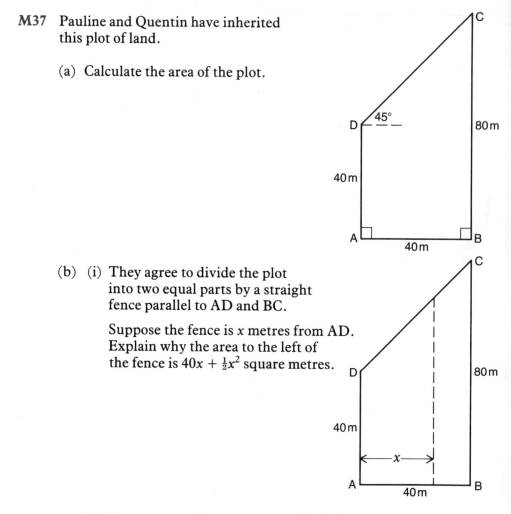

(b) (i) They agree to divide the plot into two equal parts by a straight fence parallel to AD and BC.

Suppose the fence is x metres from AD. Explain why the area to the left of the fence is $40x + \frac{1}{2}x^2$ square metres.

(ii) They want to choose x so as to divide the field as closely as possible into two equal parts. They can measure x to the nearest 0·5 m. Find by trial and error the value of x they should choose.

M38 Each shape below is made from a piece of wire of length 12 cm. Calculate the area of each shape, to the nearest 0·1 cm².

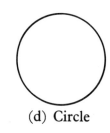

(a) Equilateral triangle

(b) Square

(c) Regular hexagon

(d) Circle